# ogham
## sketch book

## a diary of tree lore & spiritual growth

by
### Karen Cater

Illustrated by Karen Cater

Edited by
### Colin Cater

Hedingham
Fair

www.hedinghamfair.co.uk

To
Colin, Aly and Chris
who shared much of the journey

# ACKNOWLEDGEMENTS

Thanks to Colin for being there and keeping the world off my back, and whose skill with words far outweighs my own.

Thanks to my Mum whose help made it possible.

Thanks to Peter Gotto for his help and advice in the early stages.

Thanks to Dave Eckersley for his expertise.

Thanks to Brian Krengel for the use of a wonderful song.

Thanks to Pete Jennings for checking I hadn't made a fool of myself with all the Norse stuff.

Thanks to Graeme Fayers for all his encouragement, especially for teaching me how to use the Apple Mac.

Thanks above all to the Spirits of the Trees around Southey Green for sharing their Wisdom with me.

**Please note:** Herbal Remedies described in this book are for interest only. Neither the author nor the publisher can be held responsible for any adverse reactions. Readers should seek the advice of a competent health professional in cases of medical need. If anybody is taking prescribed medicines, they should consult their doctor before using any herbal remedies.

# Contents

# Introduction

I was born in Downland Sussex in 1954. As a small child, I would go with my mother on "Nature Rambles", and learnt to recognise the trees and plants, birds and animals I saw, while picking wild flowers in the spring, grasses to decorate the house in early summer, blackberries for jam in the autumn, and holly and pine cones in the winter to make Christmas decorations. If there was something we couldn't identify, we would take some home and "look it up in the book". So I grew up with an insatiable curiosity about, and fascination with the natural world. Walking to school each day across the corn fields I watched the seasons changing, knew where the different birds nested, and where the sloes grew. I built dens in the hedgerows and gradually got to know my own landscape intimately, something that I was not able to do again for many years.

As a teenager I often sang at my local folk club. I studied illustration at art school, first at St. Martin's in London, and then in Norwich where the call of the folk music pub sessions proved irresistible, till I joined an Irish band and toured Germany for a year with them. But I couldn't wait to get back to the English countryside. After Germany, I moved back to the wilds of rural North Norfolk, not far from the sea. Here I somehow ended up running a wildlife sanctuary at my home, taking in injured and oil covered birds, treating and rehabilitating them before returning them to the wild. All the while I was working as an artist, designing engravings for glass.

During the 1980s I had two children, which put many of my interests on hold, but I kept painting, sometimes commissions, often watercolours of the alleys at the back of our house, quite impressionistic and free, which I exhibited and sold. I also became interested in herbalism, working with herbs I planted in my garden. Several years and house moves later, I landed in rural North Essex, and renewed my interest in folk music, starting and running a folk club, performing and taking part in several annual customs.

Then in my early 40s an opportunity arose. Colin and I decided to take leave of the rat race and build a life based around my artwork. Hedingham Fair was born.

We set up an artist's studio, installed a printing press and I rekindled my lino cutting skills, to produce designs based initially on the mid winter folk customs of England; Mumming, Wassailing and Molly dancing, which we published as Christmas cards.

One morning, in that liminal space between waking and sleeping, I had a flash of inspiration. An image of the Green Man appeared to me, and I knew I was being sent in a new direction. Here was an image that had fascinated all sorts of people for centuries; found in medieval churches, not Christian in essence, but with a mystical quality I wanted to explore. We started visiting old churches looking for Green Men, and I became fascinated by medieval decoration generally, as it often portrayed the everyday activities of the ordinary people of the time, playing musical instruments, harvesting or dancing etc. as well as the beautiful decorative abstract designs and mythical beasts that seemed to be depicted everywhere. I produced designs for cards and t-shirts incorporating elements of these ideas and styles, which as Hedingham Fair, we sold in folk festival craft markets every summer.

Every year, at Sidmouth festival we would stay at a farm, camping in a field. Each morning the first thing we saw was a gorgeous Oak tree, most beautifully proportioned and symmetrical. I felt instinctively that I must use this image as a Tree of Life design. It took a couple of years to finalise the ideas in my head, and by this time I'd become interested in the Gods and Goddesses of ancient Britain, Neolithic burial chambers, standing stones, and other ancient, mystical and pagan ideas. The "Tree of Life" design was to depict the Wheel of the Year - the passage of the seasons, the phases of the moon, both pictorially and symbolically, so I employed a circular framework which included a series of bands with the names of the eight festivals of the Celtic year, and then, having discovered the

Tree Ogham with its symbols associated with each lunar month, these were added, all surrounding the Oak displaying the seasonal progression through the crown of the tree. (see page 66)

The following year I embarked on a major project to produce a series of cards depicting the eight festivals of the Celtic year. These were to include elements of many of the subjects I had been studying for a while now. Each image incorporated one of the ancient sites associated with the spirit of the festival; a holy well, a labyrinth, stone circles and burial chambers, and a Green Man. I used many of the relevant "correspondences", and also added animals, birds and hedgerow fruit and flowers from the appropriate seasons. To help my creative process, I carefully prepared my working environment using hypnotic music and incense to help induce an altered state of consciousness akin to meditation or trance which enabled me to work in a much freer and more intuitive way. Eventually, once the compositional drawings were completed, I cut lino blocks for each one, and painted the resulting prints in watercolour.

Having found a way of working that had produced such good results; the next project I embarked on was even more ambitious. I returned to the Ogham system of the Druids, intent on learning all about it. I was fascinated by the idea that an alphabet could also be a zodiac, a system of divination and a code linking mythology, history, mysticism, tree lore, herbalism, birds, crafts, folklore and customs, all the things I had been interested in all my life!

I bought a second hand copy of the White Goddess by Robert Graves, which gave me the raw material to work with; the Tree Alphabet, said to be "the original Druid relic transmitted orally down the centuries".

Armed with the list and order of the trees, together with the dates they rule, I had to decide how to approach the project, the *modus operandi*. I wanted to discover as much as I could, but somehow just reading other people's books and learning other people's knowledge didn't seem right. I had to find a way to make this my own, my adventure, my knowledge. Then it hit me like a thunderbolt - I live in the country, surrounded by trees, there's a plantation less than a mile away, and a tract of ancient woodland only half a mile up the lane. If I couldn't learn from the trees around me there was something seriously wrong!

I decided to take each tree in turn at its allotted time and make a magical journey, like a pilgrimage, visiting and meditating with the tree, to get a feel for the character and spirit of each one. I would cut a stick from each tree and mark it with its own Ogham symbol, for later use in divination or just as a reference to link me back to the tree's spirit as needed. I would draw and paint whatever parts of the tree occurred to me to be relevant at the time, and return throughout the year to build up a body of reference. And I would keep a diary / journal / sketchbook of everything that happened, and use the artwork in it later to make a series of designs based on each tree.

Well that was the theory, anyway. I soon found out that it wasn't going to be that easy. Firstly there's no point going tromping around the woods if you don't know what you're looking for, and though I'd invested in a good field guide to help me identify the trees I didn't already know, there was the problem of deciduous trees in winter – at this stage I wasn't able to identify them bare of leaves!

The next obstacle was a busy lifestyle; there were times when I just couldn't get to the trees at the right time because of the pressure of work and commitments away from home, and although I'd like to think otherwise, I'm not superwoman! So I had to be pragmatic about things and do what I could, when I had the time, and hope for the best. I did my journeys and kept my diary. I even did the drawings and paintings, but if you look carefully at the diary entries in each chapter of this book, you'll see that not many of the early ones were actually within the allotted period. Some of the later ones were a bit out too if I'm completely honest. However, one of the best things about this project was that at last I was able to learn my landscape all over again, just like when I was a child, to really get in touch with the land I live on, and become part of it.

When I made my journeys some odd things happened. I immediately started noticing all sorts of coincidences, as if the trees were really trying to show me something. There was a feeling that everything was as it should be and that all would be revealed in time. I can't quite explain, but if you read between the lines you may find linkages like the ones that occurred to me at the time. Eventually it seemed that several layers of meaning were operating at once, and insights into the nature of reality were almost within my grasp. I know that this may sound a bit strange, but I hope you will feel at least a bit of the reward I felt from doing this work as you read the book.

When the research work was nearly completed, and my sketchbook was filled with artwork and notes about all sorts of stuff relating to each tree or shrub I started to design the card series, and soon realized that I needed to make better sense of everything I was learning.

The first problem related to the dating of the trees. Some sources gave standard calendar dates starting from 24th December. Others used lunar months starting with the first new moon after the 23rd December, which would obviously change each year. As I was designing cards for sale over a (hopefully) longish period, regularly changing dates were inappropriate, so no problem in solving that one then! I used the standardized dates.

Then there was the issue about which particular tree or shrub to portray for some of the months, as sources again disagreed. This time I went with my own environment, and there was only one obvious choice in each case, as I explain in the chapters on Bramble, Wheatstraw and White Poplar.

Setting about the final artwork for the 21 cards was the scariest bit, but when I actually came to it, I had been working with the trees so long that their characters had become familiar and all sorts of design issues had already been settled in my head. I had a clear idea of the colour scheme for each design in mind before I even really thought about it, suggested by the trees themselves.

I drew a template for all the cards based on Celtic illuminated manuscript styles. I then dropped in the different elements of each tree's design; the central image was the main tree illustration, a branch showing leaves and flowers or fruit. Immediately above and below I put the name of the tree in English and in the Ogham language. Placed in the top left corner was the Ogham symbol, on the right, the dates to which it referred, while the bottom left and right corners held an image from appropriate mythology or folklore, and an illustration of another aspect of the tree itself. The design to the centre left and right of every card is taken from the Book of Kells, and is called the "Tree of Life", which emerges from a pot decorated with the Triscel, symbol of life, sometimes called the "Wheel of the Sun". These concepts can also be seen on the front cover of this book.

In no time at all I had drawn the complete series and only had to paint them. Then I wrote notes for the backs, based on the research done already, including a paragraph describing the Ogham that came to me, complete, in the middle of the night, which I had to get up to write down before it was lost! Soon the cards were launched and received with some enthusiasm by our customers that year. Then someone suggested I should write a book using the sketchbook as the basis.

Again I thought this would be a fairly pain free exercise, as the work had all been done…wrong! I could never have imagined how much more I had to learn! All the notes had to be rewritten as most of it I'd written in a sort of note form, almost shorthand, and everything needed expanding. Then the book took on a life of its own. Each chapter started to develop its own individual character. This process gradually became more pronounced as things progressed, until by the time I reached the last section, the vowels, I had got to the stage where I almost sat at the computer and let the book write itself. I began to think that perhaps there was something working through me and I was no more than the instrument of this outpouring….something.

The knowledge and insights I've gained from this work have led me to continue working with tree imagery, some of the newer designs are here too. It seems as if there is a bottomless well of inspiration and the learning goes on . . .

# Ogham
## The Wisdom of the Trees

In ancient times, our Celtic Druid ancestors devised a system, part alphabet (the Beith-Luis-Nion), part calendar/zodiac, which could be carved, using simple notches, onto wood or stone. Each character was a number and a letter. The consonants were time periods, mostly Lunar months, and the vowels were the solstices or equinoxes. Each symbol represented a tree or shrub, around which grew an extensive mythology, recording historical and religious stories, the uses of each tree both for craftwork and medicinally, and a divinatory system similar to the Tarot.

To the Celts, the whole landscape was alive with meaning, and wisdom - the wisdom of the trees.

## The Tree Wheel of the Year

The outer ring of the wheel (left) shows all the trees in their proper positions as far as possible - the Solstices and Equinoxes are positioned between trees that include the actual date, and as close as possible to the proper position. Apple and Blackthorn form the inner ring as they rule the light and dark halves of the year, changing at Mayday and Halloween. The centre of the wheel is the "day" of "a year and a day". The Celtic lunar calendar reckoned the year in thirteen months of 28 days = 364 days, so to complete the year an extra day was added, ruled by Mistletoe, the most magical of all.

| Symbol | Letter | Name | Dates | Interpretation | No. |
|--------|--------|------|-------|----------------|-----|
| ⊢ | B | Beith<br>Birch | 24th Dec – 20th Jan<br>1st Lunar month | New Beginnings<br>Start of a Journey | 1 |
| ⊨ | L | Luis<br>Rowan | 21st Jan – 17th Feb<br>2nd Lunar month | Quickening<br>Magic | 2 |
| ⊫ | N | Nion<br>Ash | 18th Feb – 17th Mar<br>3rd Lunar month | World Tree<br>Yggdrasil | 3 |
| ⊬ | F | Fearn<br>Alder | 18th Mar – 14th Apr<br>4thLunar month | Chief<br>Oracular Singing Head | 4 |
| ⊭ | S | Saille<br>Willow | 15th Apr – 12th May<br>5th Lunar month | Loss, Grief, Flexibility<br>Visionary Dreams | 5 |
| ⊢ | H | Huath<br>Hawthorn | 13th May – 9th Jun<br>6th Lunar month | Fertility<br>Caution | 6 |
| = | D | Duir<br>Oak | 10th Jun – 7th Jul<br>7th Lunar month | Door<br>Thunder King | 7 |
| ≡ | T | Tinne<br>Holly | 8th Jul – 4th Aug<br>8th Lunar month | Spear<br>Protection | 8 |
| ≣ | C | Coll<br>Hazel | 5th Aug – 1st Sep<br>9th Lunar month | Inspiration<br>Wisdom | 9 |
| ≣ | Q | Quert<br>Apple | The Light half<br>of the Year | The Magical Island in the West<br>Love , Immortality | 10 |

| | | | | |
|---|---|---|---|---|
| M | Muin Bramble | 2nd Sep - 29th Sep 10th lunar month | Connections Joy, Intoxication | 11 |
| G | Gort Ivy | 30th Sep - 27thOct 11th lunar month | Struggle, Climb Transformation | 12 |
| Ng | Ngetal Wheatstraw | 28th Oct - 24th Nov 12th lunar month | Established Power Fleeting Nature of Authority | 13 |
| St | Straif Blackthorn | The Dark half of the Year | Strength to Overcome Adversity | 14 |
| R | Ruis Elder | 25th Nov - 22nd Dec 13th lunar month | Real Wisdom The Crone | 15 |
| | - Mistletoe | 23rd Dec - the "day" of "a year and a day" | Liminal Space The Golden Bough | |
| A | Ailm Scots Pine | 22nd Dec Winter Solstice at the start of the year | A Signpost at the Beginning of the Journey | 16 |
| O | Onn Gorse | 21st March Spring Equinox | Beware Ungoverned Passion Corruption | 17 |
| U | Ur Heather | 21st June Summer Solstice | Solitude Encounter with the Divine | 18 |
| E | Eadha White Poplar | 21st September Autumn Equinox | Communication with the Divine | 19 |
| I | Ioho Yew | 21st Dec Winter Solstice at the end of the year | Culmination of the Cycle of Life, Death and Regeneration | 20 |

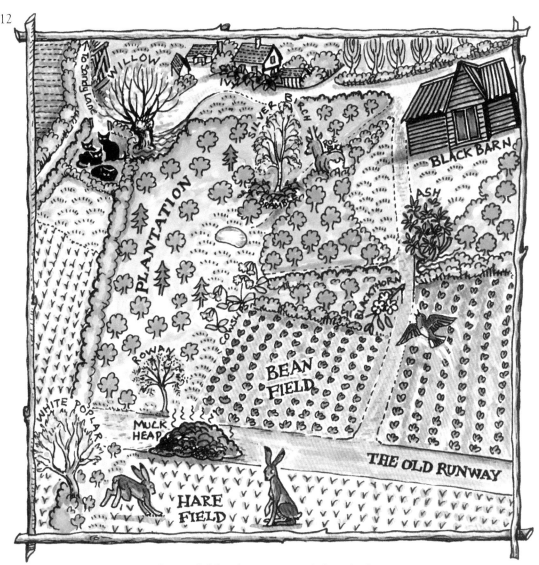

*The Airfield, Plantation and the Black Barn*

*Southey Green, Sunnyside, Hill Farm and Lightfoot*

*The Broaks*

*Sible, Alderford Mill, the Shops and School*

# BIRCH - BEITH

Letter - B
Number - 1
Rules - 24th December to 20th January
1st Lunar month

## Correspondences
Element - Water
Planet - Moon
Gender - Feminine
Bird - Pheasant, Partridge
Deities - Frigg, Venus

## Interpretation
Early beginnings (poss. false beginning)
Check information is correct then proceed -
when you are right you will know
Clear away old patterns to make way
for new ones - CHANGE
Losing fear of unknown
Cleansing, journey
Birth, rebirth
New ideas, opportunities

Birch

24th Dec to 20th Jan

Beith

# Birch t

23rd January, Friday, mid day.
Cold, overcast, south-westerly breeze.
It's been raining for days, and the
land is sodden. New moon.
My first pilgrimage in search of the
wisdom of the trees, I'm a little
apprehensive. I decided not to research
before this journey, just to see what
happens and what I can interpret
without any prior expectations - a test really
both of me and of the trees, will I feel the ancient
wisdom? Today I'm looking for Birch, a bit late,
but it's the first day it's been dry enough to
get out onto the land for ages. I walked
down the lane. What's that tree growing
by the path dividing the patch of
boggy land from Malcolm's pond?

# Beith

**24th Dec to 20th Jan**

**1st lunar month**
Beth B 1

The bark is pale, but not white, with shoots growing from lumpy nodes all the way up the trunk.

I carefully cut a shoot to take home to identify, then walked on, and turned in to the plantation at the Black Barn, taking the diagonal path into the trees. A hundred yards in was a slender tree, delicate elegant, with pure white bark that shone out in the gloom like a beacon. Definitely Silver Birch – Beith. The path was wet, mud stuck to my boots, a bramble snatched at my leg and I nearly tripped, I stopped to unhook it from my jeans and thought – maybe I should have asked the tree first. After that it was easy, my change of mindset had opened my awareness and I felt I was accepted. I stood there just looking at the lovely bark, like parchment, with the rich red-brown of emerging branches, still bearing the remains of last years catkins, but already showing the early signs of this years growth. I took the lowest branch to make my first Ogham stick, and thanking Beith made my way home.

# The Lady of the Woods

B eith, "The Lady of the Woods", is the first tree to colonise wilderness, and it is fitting that she is the first tree in the Ogham alphabet, and signifies beginnings. When I returned from my first journey to the trees, I began by writing up my diary and recording as much detail as possible about the trip, weather conditions, time, moon phase etc. Once I had done this, I started to research the correspondences, and was amazed to discover that much of what I was reading had parallels with what I had written. I wondered if at some time in the dim and distant past, the Druids who had devised this system using trees, sought significances at the start of the year which to them suggested Birch, so when I looked for Birch I found the same ideas that had spoken to the Druids. Is this what is meant by an ancient truth?

Was it just coincidence? Or was I being guided, recruited even, to do this work? I certainly felt that, having been successfully on track with the Birch journey, I would continue with renewed enthusiasm in my search of the wisdom of the trees.

Obviously, this was the beginning of a new project, but I had quite arbitrarily started on a Friday- Frigg's day, and it was a new moon! The land was saturated with puddles everywhere, and birch's element is water.

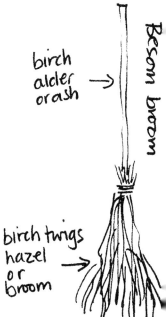

birch alder or ash →

Besom broom

birch twigs hazel or broom →

To clean my hearth, I use a handbrush with the name Frigg, the home loving Norse goddess who is associated with the hearth, carved in runes on the handle. In the same way a handful of Birch twigs was probably used in ancient times to clear the hearth and keep the living space clean in the caves and huts of our ancestors.

Birch twigs are still used to make besom brooms, and the handles can be made of birch, alder or ash. The traditional "witches Broomstick" is a bridge, as she "flies" between the mundane world and the spirit realm.

"Birching" as cleansing, is to drive out evil influences, to renew and make clean.

"Beating the bounds" is a custom designed to reinforce the memory of a parish (or tribal) boundary, and is performed by walking the boundary and hitting markers; gates, milestones, trees, etc. with birch rods, occasionally even upending a young lad and bouncing him - he'll certainly remember the spot where that happened!

Hard tough and flexible wood used
for wheels, interior woodwork and
fuel.
Bark as parchment, and used in
dressing skins.
Sap - collected in spring,
fermented to make beer, wine,
spirits and vinegar.
For treatment of kidney stones and
bladder problems and as a
mouthwash
Tonic from wood and bark -
diuretic and laxative, reduces
inflammation and pain.

V. yellow pollen

April

Seeds
←————————→
last yr's
catkin

Bark on main trunk - white, papery, but
on branches - rich warm reddish brown,
smooth. Still bearing catkins from last
summer. Seeds - small, winged, spread
great distances.

Next door to the house I grew up in, there
was a Silver Birch tree, and every year
there were seeds in the house, they got
everywhere! I often collected them and
kept them in a matchbox.

# ROWAN - LUIS

Letter - L
Number - 2
Rules - 21st January to 17th February
2nd Lunar month

## Correspondences

Element - Fire
Planet - Moon
Gender - Feminine
Bird - Duck
Deities - Penelope; Lugh, God of fire & the Sun

## Interpretation

Tree of life, first consciousness
Magical protection
Peaceful rest

## Country Names

Quicken tree
Quickbeam
Witchen tree

Rowan

21ˢᵗ Jan
to
17ᵗʰ Feb

Luis

# ROWAN

14th April, early afternoon, sunny, mild, light SW wind. Waxing moon. It's been a long time since my last journey, not through lack of motivation, but it's the turn of Rowan next and that's a problem; it's deciduous, so till now there's been no leaves to identify it by.

Today I made my way to the plantation, again by the Black Barn path. As I passed through the gate I saw a Roebuck browsing among the shrubs just off the path, ten yards ahead of me. He saw me instantly, turned, and bobbed away into the bramble thicket with a flash of white rump, leaving me standing spellbound. I followed his trail and glimpsed him again, he was leading me deeper

# LUIS

**Jan 21st to Feb 17th**

quickentree
quickbeam

into the plantation where the paths disappeared and the going was more difficult. Pushing my way through the undergrowth I emerged and came face to face with Beith. I took the opportunity to cut a small twig with fresh new catkins to draw when I got back to the studio, and thanking her, moved on. I headed back to the path around the beanfield where suddenly I stopped and caught my breath at the sight of a carpet of cowslips spreading into the grass all around in great magical drifts. Following the path I finally came back to the concrete runway and approached a young Rowan, which stood at the meeting of the wood and the cultivated land. Now it was possible to identify by the soft green leaves starting to uncurl and buds forming with the promise of blossom. The whole world is bursting with new life.

# Quicken Tree

*Rowan from the Norse "Runa"- a charm.*
*The Celtic name is "fid na ndruad" - the wizard's tree.*

Rowan is also called Quicken tree, Quickbeam and Witchen tree. Quick is an old word for life, as in "the quick and the dead". Quickening is the term used to describe the first feeling of movement of a baby in the womb, the first sign of life. So as the Birch tree is the start, the clearing away for the new, so Rowan is the tree of new life.

Every new life is precious and must be protected, so an amulet of a cross or a hoop of Rowan twigs tied with red thread - the colour of life - and hung on the cradle will protect and prevent a baby being stolen by the Feare folk (fairies).

A Rowan branch hung over the door will protect a house from evil, and Rowan trees growing beside springs or wells are said to repel evil spirits.

Rowan twigs hung above a bed will prevent nightmares and disturbed sleep.

The Welsh believe that a Rowan tree planted in a churchyard will protect the spirits of those that are buried there and stop their ghosts from walking.

*"Peace be here and Rowan tree."-* Celtic blessing.

An amulet of a cross or a
hoop of Rowan twigs tied with
red thread - the colour of life -
and hung on the cradle will
prevent a baby being stolen by
the Feare folk

Rowan is called "Mountain Ash" as it grows higher
on the mountains than any other tree, and it has
paired, opposite and serrated leaves like the Ash.
Wood used for tools, pegs, poles, longbows,
wands, staffs, and knife blades.

early
October
← !
FIRE!

# Rowan Luis

Serrated paired leaflets

light + delicate appearance from distance

buds push thru' open flowers to bloom in front

blackish dark buds

smooth bark on twigs

## ROWAN JELLY

High in Vitamin C
half lb Rowan berries
1lb crab or cooking apples, chopped
2 or 3 slices of fresh ginger
half a sliced lemon

Just cover rowan and apples with cold water, add ginger and lemon. Simmer till the fruit is pulped. Pour into a jelly bag or a sieve lined with muslin and leave to drip overnight into a large pan. Don't squeeze as this makes it cloudy.
To 1pt juice add 1lb sugar, boil till setting point is reached.
Pour into sterilized jars.
Rowan jelly has a strong flavour that goes well with duck and game.

# ASH - NION

Letter - N
Number - 3
Rules - 18th February to 17th March
3rd Lunar month

## Correspondences

Element - Water
Planet - Sun
Gender - both Male & Female
changeable (male dominant)
Bird - Snipe
Deity - Odin

## Interpretation

Cosmic tree - Yggdrasil
Linking, connections
Transformation
The great pattern
Web of Wyrd

Ash

18ᵗʰ Feb
to
17ᵗʰ Mar

Nion

# ASH

17th May, Hot, sunny, blue sky, SUMMER!
Skylarks singing over the fields, baby birds
everywhere, Starlings using our garden as
a nursery. I'd been thinking about making
my Ash journey for several weeks, and I
hadn't had the time, or was I putting it
off? The Ash trees had finished flowering,
the fluffy-tassles had turned into bunches
of seed pods (keys) but the branches on the
mature trees in the lane were too high to
reach for gathering. I walked with Colin
past the barn to the airfield and along the
path where I noticed for the first time
young Ash trees in the first stretch of
hedgerow (remember this for

NION

the return journey). In the field the
beans were in full bloom, the scent was strong,
sweet like perfume, and I remarked how quiet
it was, "not a lark to be heard, maybe they don't
nest among beans". As soon as the words left
my mouth a skylark leapt up almost at our
feet and climbed into the air singing as
sweet as the beanflowers she'd been
sitting among. — Wrong again - guard my
tongue, watch and learn!
On the way back Colin had to jump to
reach a branch for me to cut, then further
down the lane we found some within easy
reach. Perhaps I must learn not to
jump to conclusions, wait and check the
facts, be still and the truth will become clear.

# Connections and Interpretations

In many mythologies all over the world, the tree is the World Axis, and represents the ultimate reality, inexhaustible life and immortality. It is one of the most fundamental of all traditional symbols, its form reflecting the threefold mystery of life, with roots that originate in the underworld, the trunk standing in the middle-earth of our physical existence, and the branches reaching up to the heavens, the world beyond.

In Norse tradition, Yggdrasil, a vast Ash tree, is the framework upon which all reality hangs, and it supports the universe, linking the realms of Gods, men, giants

and spirits. Yggdrasil has come to represent the great pattern of life, the Web of Wyrd, in which all things are interconnected, physical and spiritual, natural and magical. It links the three circles of existence - past, present and future - but you can't always see how. Sometimes truth takes time to become clear.

The tree also appears as a symbol of transformation in several mythologies, and as a means by which transformation may be achieved. The Norse God Odin hung for nine days from Yggdrasil to gain divine knowledge and learn the secrets of the runes, which he carved on a spear cut from one of its branches.

Jesus, crucified on a tree, overcame death and was transformed to become the Christian Saviour of the world. The Buddha meditated beneath a tree to gain enlightenment, offering his followers pathways to Nirvana. The Jewish Quabbalah or Tree of Life provides a framework for meditation on the understanding of the divine infinite also expressing the potential for spiritual growth inherent in all living beings, that with a solid grounding in the earth of our ancestors, and nourished by the inspiration of ideas falling like leaves to enrich that earth, we will develop and grow like the tallest tree until we reach the stars.

*Odin hung on Yggdrasil to gain the knowledge of the Runes*

It seems that these mythologies have diverse purposes and can be viewed at many different levels, superficially they are entertaining stories. At a slightly deeper level, the tales of the ancients are instructional, influencing thought and behaviour - the moral fable. In the hands of the unscrupulous, myths can be used to manipulate others for political ends. However, if one looks a little further and meditates on these stories, they may eventually begin to see beneath the surface to deeper, archetypal meanings - concepts that have fundamental significance.

Look at it this way, in our earth-bound existence, we find it difficult to conceive of the vastness and complexity of concepts such as the "universe" and "the spirit realm". Depending on where you're standing, the Universe might be viewed physically at any point on a spectrum between micro and macro. Imagine a world populated by beings made up of molecules, each molecule is a tiny universe, populated by beings made up of molecules.. and so on ad infinitum, in both directions, larger and smaller. That's just the physical realm!

What happens on the spiritual plane? Where is each individual's place within the great pattern of life? Imagine again, each person like a spider at the centre of their own web, now connect all the webs together so that they form a huge network, with each individual person, animal, plant, interconnected to every other individual ...by now your head will probably be spinning! The good thing is that the web is real, if we can only forget the mundane for a moment and expand our consciousness to take in just a bit of it!

It would be possible to consider ourselves as totally insignificant in all this vastness, but this would be to miss the point, because to remove one link is to change the pattern, so we are all as important as each other!

Now isn't that exciting?

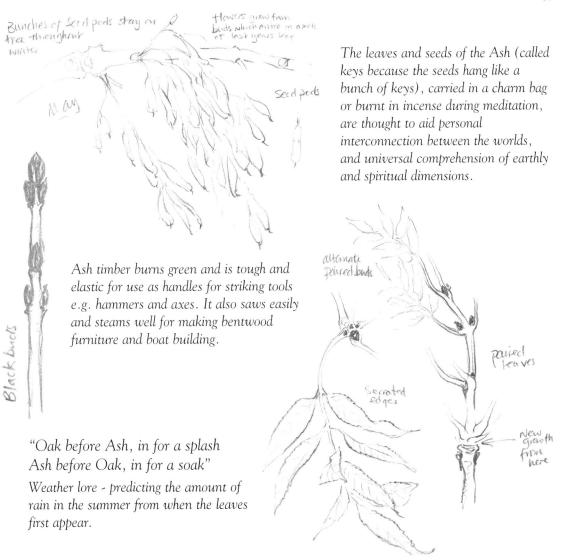

Bunches of seed pods stay on tree throughout winter

Flowers grow from buds which arise in axels of last years bud

May

Seed pods

The leaves and seeds of the Ash (called keys because the seeds hang like a bunch of keys), carried in a charm bag or burnt in incense during meditation, are thought to aid personal interconnection between the worlds, and universal comprehension of earthly and spiritual dimensions.

Black buds

alternate paired buds

paired leaves

serrated edges

New growth from here

Ash timber burns green and is tough and elastic for use as handles for striking tools e.g. hammers and axes. It also saws easily and steams well for making bentwood furniture and boat building.

"Oak before Ash, in for a splash
Ash before Oak, in for a soak"

Weather lore - predicting the amount of rain in the summer from when the leaves first appear.

# ALDER - FEARN

Letter - F
Number - 4
Rules - 18th March to 14th April
4th Lunar month

**Correspondences**
Element - Water
Planet - Venus
Gender - Masculine
Bird - Raven
Deities - Bran the Blessed

**Interpretation**
Oracular head
Singing head
Protection of the Nation

**Country Names**
Owler
"Ealdor", old English = chief

Alder

18th Mar
to
14th Apr

Fearn

10th June. Mid morning, warm, Corpus Christi,
2 days since transit of Venus, waning moon.
I had been looking for Alder for weeks,
none on the Plantation, none on the lane,
I'd seen some while out driving in several
places, but nowhere I could park, and
anyway, it wouldn't be the same if it came
from outside 'my patch'! It was becoming
obvious I'd have to look slightly further afield.
Driving to Alderford Mill on the road to Sible,
I narrowly missed a blackbird who flew in front
of the van. I tried to reach an Alder 'carr' on
the riverbank in a field surrounded by
electric fences and barbed wire,
but I couldn't get near. So I
traced the river along
into the village,
and found a

# fearn 4th lunar month Alder

path behind the shop, between the houses that led down to the river bank, all overgrown with nettles. There were blackbirds rooting around on the ground, throwing up leaf litter in their search for insects, and also in the trees chasing each other from branch to branch, making scolding cries. That's when I finally noticed that I was in fact standing under a tall old Alder, and I could have sworn he was laughing at the merry dance he'd led me! There were several trunk like limbs, one of which had broken over, and new whippy stems were growing from the base, the shield shaped leaves were very distinctive with a concave tip, smooth and leathery, and soft new green cones were starting to replace last year's crumbly brown ones. When I got home and did my research, I found that the bird sacred to Alder is the Raven, a very large black bird – we don't get Ravens in Essex, but we certainly get plenty of black birds!

# In Search of Alder

There were many times during my year learning about the Ogham when I found it impossible to make a journey at exactly the right time for the tree I was studying. This was one - and I really didn't want to make do with an Alder tree from miles away just because I hadn't found one yet. It was important to me that I was also learning about my home ground, making connection with my own place, becoming one with my surroundings, part of the landscape. I should have known that something would turn up - then I remembered Alderford Mill just down the road, the name was a bit of a giveaway! Why hadn't I thought of it before? Probably because I just wasn't ready.

Alderford Mill

# Bran the Blessed

*Alder from Old English "Ealdor" = chief*

Another of the many purposes of mythology is encoding history, telling of battles between gods and heroes, which record the overthrow of one ancient tribe by another. It can also hold the key to more practical secrets, as in the epic tale of Bran.

The Alder is sacred to Bran the Blessed, giant chief from the Welsh "Mabinogion" cycle. Bran used his body to span the river Linon and his men crossed over using his body as a bridge. Ever since, alder pilings have been used for bridge footings as the oily wood is water resistant, and when used as underwater foundations it does not rot.

After Bran's death his followers cut off his head (as he had told them to) and the head continued to prophesy and sing. In the same way, the top branches of Alder trees which have since been used to make magical flutes, for use in ritual and ceremony.

Eventually Bran's head was carried to the White Mount, later the Tower of London, and buried. Here it was said to protect Britain from invasion, and as long as Bran's sacred Ravens remain at the Tower, Britain will be safe.

This belief, derived from ancient mythology is still currently held fast, and can be seen to this day, as the Ravens kept at the Tower of London are pinioned - they have their wings clipped to prevent them from flying away.

# WILLOW - SAILLE

Letter - S
Number - 5
Rules - 15th April to 12th May
5th Lunar month

**Correspondences**
Element - Water
Planet - Moon
Metal - Silver
Gender - Feminine
Bird - Swan
Beast - Hare
Deities - Crone aspect of Triple Goddess

**Interpretation**
Sorrow, loss
Flexibility, adaptability
Wisdom gained from adversity and experience

Willow

15th Apr
to
12th May

Saille

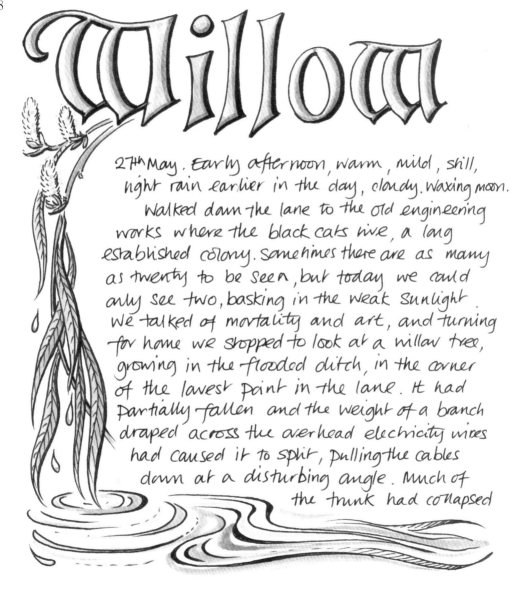

# Willow

27th May. Early afternoon, warm, mild, still, light rain earlier in the day, cloudy. Waxing moon.

Walked down the lane to the old engineering works where the black cats live, a long established colony. Sometimes there are as many as twenty to be seen, but today we could only see two, basking in the weak sunlight. We talked of mortality and art, and turning for home we stopped to look at a willow tree, growing in the flooded ditch, in the corner of the lowest point in the lane. It had partially fallen and the weight of a branch draped across the overhead electricity wires had caused it to split, pulling the cables down at a disturbing angle. Much of the trunk had collapsed

# Saille

15th April to 12th May

5th lunar month

into the water and new growth was
emerging from the wreckage of the old tree.
it was as if this willow had been naturally
coppiced. I broke off a branch, cracking it easily,
as it was attached to the trunk by no more than
a thin core of connective tissue. 
The long slender leaves were shiny green
above, silvery white below, and radiated
in a spiral from the branches. I thought of
the correspondences associated with willow -
water, moon, female cycle, loss, pain, sorrow,
flexible, adaptable, sleep, dreams, regeneration,
rebirth - And I was beginning to understand
the wisdom that the trees were offering to me.
The connections were starting to form a
three-dimensional map in my head, where every
concept and every experience has its
allotted place, a rough guide to the
ever turning wheel of life.

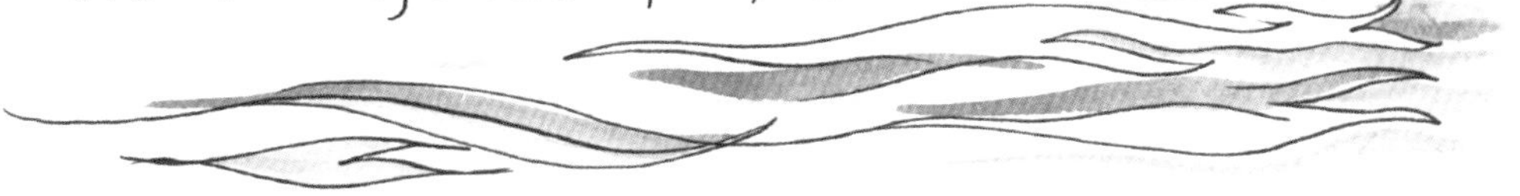

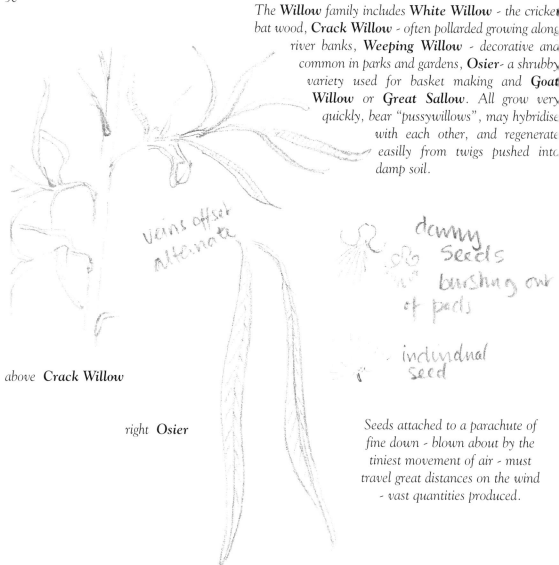

The **Willow** family includes **White Willow** - the cricket bat wood, **Crack Willow** - often pollarded growing along river banks, **Weeping Willow** - decorative and common in parks and gardens, **Osier**- a shrubby variety used for basket making and **Goat Willow** or **Great Sallow**. All grow very quickly, bear "pussywillows", may hybridise with each other, and regenerate easilly from twigs pushed into damp soil.

veins offset alternate

damny seeds bushing out of pods

indivdnal seed

*above* **Crack Willow**

*right* **Osier**

Seeds attached to a parachute of fine down - blown about by the tiniest movement of air - must travel great distances on the wind - vast quantities produced.

# Weeping Willow

Willow, to me, is probably the most archetypal feminine tree in the Ogham. With her silvery leaves she is associated with the Moon, whose gravitational pull upon the waters of the earth causes the tides and regulates the female cycle, and also has a clear affect on the mood swings of those who are most sensitive to her influence.

> "All around my hat I will wear the green willow
> All for my true love who is far, far away."

This traditional song shows that the willow tree has long been associated with sorrow, loss and mourning, growing beside pools of tears, reflecting on the transience of life. The swan ascending, symbol of the released spirit, joins the moon and stars in the heavens, but the cycle of life continues as fresh shoots emerge from the waters below, and a dragonfly dries his newly opened wings and prepares to take flight into new life.

# Sweet Dreams

Night time and sleep are Willow's province; the downy seeds of Willow trees were used to stuff pillows, which was said to aid sleep and connection with the other world for visionary dreams. In classical times, priests and priestesses would sleep in Willow groves to obtain eloquence and prophetic and oracular visions.

## To make Vision Water

Charge spring water, by placing it in a clear glass on a windowsill where the light of the full moon will shine on it most of the night. In the morning, light a bundle of 5 or 7 willow wands and plunge them, still burning, into the charged water. This may be kept for one lunar month and used to aid clairvoyance and visionary work by bathing the eyes and massaging into the forehead (3rd eye).

*Weeping Willow leaves and flowers - March*

As sleep dulls the pain of loss, a decoction of willow bark will relieve pain, fever and inflammation, and is the source of the aspirin taken to relieve a headache. After adversity and loss, the willow encourages flexibility of nature and spirit.

As a twig cut from willow will root if planted into damp soil, so we move on from one period of life to a new era - adaptable, but with wisdom gained from experience, which is the wisdom of the Crone, the wise woman.

alternate

May

Willow is flexible, and by coppicing - cutting the tree down to ground level - long stems regenerate from the base as if by magic, which when cut and softened by soaking in water, may be used to create baskets and cradles.

Neolithic man constructed woven willow pathways which stretched for miles across boggy land, and discovered that willow charcoal provided a wonderful medium for drawing, giving the means by which dreams and visions could be recorded and shared.

*Goat Willow or Great Sallow*

# HAWTHORN - HUATH

Letter - H
Number - 6
Rules - 13th May to 9th June
6th Lunar month

## Correspondences
Element - Fire
Time - Sunrise
Planet - Mars
Gender - Feminine
Bird - Crow
Deities - Maiden aspect of Triple Goddess
Flora, Blodeuwedd

## Interpretation
The coming of summer
Purity, chastity, innocence
Preparation

## Country names
Whitethorn
Maythorn
"Haegthorn"- Saxon = hedgetree

1

hawthorn

13th May
to
9th June

huathe

# hawthorn 1

1st May. Dawn, clear, a beautiful rosy sunrise. According to Old Bob down at Hill Farm, legend tells that Henry VIII kept a pack of hounds at Sonthey Green for hunting deer, and each of the local fields was named after one of his hounds. Opposite our house is a field called 'Lightfoot', which is separated from the lane by a Hawthorn hedge, cut back annually between harvest and Ploughing. It is dense, stunted and low, and forms an impenetrable barrier. The Mayblossom here grows in great profusion. Every Mayday morning I get up before dawn to watch the sun rising across the valley, and to wash my face in the morning dew. It is here in the gateway, under the Oak tree that I stand. A magical time, All the world is still asleep, except me, the wood pigeons, and this year a fallow doe who stopped to watch me from twenty yards up the lane, I could almost see her wondering what

# huathe

night I had to be there, humans should all be abed at this time in the morning! As the light grows and the dawn chorus builds, I sing the old Mayday songs and pick sprays of hawthorn to weave a garland to hang on the door in celebration of the coming of Summer. In 1752 the new Gregorian calendar was introduced, recasting the dates and removing eleven days. But old ways die hard, and people still refer to "old" Mayday – the 12th, eleven days after May 1st.

If old Mayday is the ancient festival of the coming of Summer, then the first day of the month of hawthorn is the first day of Summer. It is also exactly the time the hawthorn blossom appears!

# Mayday - the coming of Summer

I have always associated Hawthorn with the coming of summer. Although Mayday (Beltane) has long been celebrated on May 1st, is this the real time for Mayday or should it be May 12th? Should we reckon it by the old Julian calendar or the new Gregorian calendar adopted in England in 1752? In ancient times young girls a-Maying went on May Day eve, gathering May boughs in blossom. Such occurrences are now nigh impossible as the Hawthorn does not blossom in many parts of England until Mid May (just in time for May Day under the old system).

Perhaps it would be better to take our cue from where we live and watch for the signs of summer, which vary slightly from year to year, and place to place? Well, yes, that's a nice idea, but not always as easy as it seems in a world so ruled by work, dates and timetables. I celebrate at dawn on the 1st May by the current calendar; at home when it falls midweek, and at Rochester Sweeps or Upton upon Severn festivals with the Morris dancers, if it falls at a weekend. Although there is hardly any May blossom out, I can celebrate again at the London Beltane Bash on Spring Bank Holiday at the end of May, when blossom is in abundance!

*Beltane Bash, Pagan Pride Parade*

The old country way of welcoming the summer on May morning was for the unmarried young people to spend the night in the woods, gathering Hawthorn boughs, which were carried into the village at dawn, and paraded with singing from house to house to bring a blessing for the fertility of the land that year, and to wish good luck to the inhabitants. This sort of activity provided a perfect opportunity for plenty of courting and horseplay with no responsible adult to interfere. Consequently it was not unexpected that a rash of weddings would follow, and a population boom nine months later! Children born as a consequence of "going a-Maying" were considered lucky and blessed.

In Victorian times, May festivities became attacked as "licentious", a strange development for a festival designed to continue family and community life within every village. This was probably a reaction against anti-social behaviour, a consequence of increasingly urban living, with cities ever since Hogarth's day soaked in Gin and Syphilis. Paradoxically we have the Victorians also to thank for the fact that May blossom is now associated with purity, chastity and innocence, as they reinvented what they perceived to be "Pagan" practices as sweet little games for children, doing away with any whiff of impropriety. Certainly Maypole dancing in its present form, with primary school girls weaving ribbons as they dance, dressed in white frocks and crowned with garlands of flowers dates from this period!

egend tells that, after the death of Jesus, Joseph of Arimathea came to Glastonbury, and planted his staff of Lebanese Hawthorn on Wearyall Hill, where in struck root and grew. It flowers every year at Christmas and a branch is sent to the Queen.

The Saxon name "heagthorn" - "hedge tree" - reveals Hawthorn's protective uses. If cut back annually, it will become a dense, stock proof hedge, and will provide edging for the field and homes to many small mammals and safe nesting places for birds.

*"Beware the Oak, it courts a stroke,*
*Beware the Ash, it courts a flash,*
*Creep under the Thorn,*
*it will save you from harm."*

If allowed to grow into a tree, Hawthorn's protective powers are said to be a bit more spiritual. Farmsteads often had a Hawthorn as a guardian tree, and it is said that to cut down a Hawthorn tree is to invite catastrophe. A thorn tree with three trunks growing from one root is called a "Faerie thorn" and is considered to be an entrance to the other world, and particularly magical as a source of spiritual protection.

Francis Bacon said in 1627 that the plague had the scent of May flowers, so it was considered to be desperately unlucky to bring Hawthorn blossom into the house, as it appeared to be inviting death into the home. A belief that is still firmly held to this day, though it is now thought of as merely bad luck.

GLASTONBURY holy Thorn

A globe would be woven from hawthorn twigs at New Year, and hung in the rafters of the kitchen to protect the house from fire. The following year, before the new amulet was made, the old one was taken down and burnt, and the ashes scattered on the ploughed fields for fertility.

Thorn trees growing beside springs and wells were often called Clouty trees, becoming places of pilgrimage, and the recipients of votive offerings and prayers for healing, where sufferers hang ribbons and trinkets in hope of a cure. The combination of spring water and hawthorn can be seen as a powerful healing source, as a tisane or a tincture, hawthorn is used as a heart tonic, and it has been demonstrated that its balancing effect means it can be used to either stimulate or suppress the cardiac and circulatory system, for the treatment of high blood pressure, palpitations and angina.

Spirit of Grain, Haw of Thorn,
Cleanse the Vein, the Blood to Speed,
By Night and Morn,
By Wood and Weed.

*"Cast ne'er a clout till May be out"*
*but does it mean the month or the flowers?*

# OAK - DUIR

Letter - D
Number - 7
Rules - 10th June to 7th July
7th Lunar month

**Correspondences**
Element - Fire
Time - Thursday
Planet - Jupiter
Gender - Masculine
Bird - Wren
Beast - Stag
Deities - Zeus, Jupiter, Thor - all Thunder Gods
Cernunnos and Herne

**Interpretation**
Sovereignty, Power
Door to inner strength and spirituality
Protection
As above, so below

Oak

10th June
to
7th July

Duir

# Oak

10th June
to
7th July

1st July, Thursday. 8.30pm Moonrise, full moon. dusk approaching. It had been a hot, stormy afternoon. I had watched the lightning in the distance from my studio, while thunder rolled around the valley. Now it was cooler and showery, a gentle breeze barely moved the leaves on the trees opposite my window. I walked to the gate into Lightfoot, to the Oak tree that had shared my vigil on May morning and again at dawn on Midsummer's day, when he seemed to shiver at the sight of the sunrise on the last day of the Oak King's reign. Standing there, I tried to imagine the concept of time as experienced by an oak tree, whose life could

# 7th lunar month DUIR

span as much as four hundred years. My visits
would be like the momentary buzz of an insect, as
he stood there watching the days and seasons come
and go. What is the nature of consciousness
of a tree? There is a most definite aura - you
can feel an edge, a boundary, as you approach a
tree, like a human's personal space, and a change
of atmosphere as you enter it, giving an impression
of character. Which is why I always now ask
permission to enter, well you wouldn't just barge
in to someone's bedroom uninvited!
I pulled down a branch, but it was hard
to cut, and the wood just inside the bark
had a red, bloody colour. I felt I should
leave an offering in return, part of
myself. A hair - a hard-earned grey
one - I plucked one, my pain for the
trees pain, tied it loosely round the cut
branch. I thanked him, and returned
thoughtfully home.

# Tree of Life

The central image of the Oak tree shows the effect of the seasons upon the cycle of life, starting with spring and birds nesting in the branches on the left, the full foliage at mid summer, and the squirrel burying acorns under the falling leaves of autumn, while winter hides the sleeping fox among the roots. Around the tree are rings showing the seasonal festivals of the Celtic peoples, the phases of the moon and the Ogham zodiac, all surrounded by the design known as the "Tree of Life" from the Book of Kells, sprouting from a pot decorated with the Triscel, sign of the Sun, the source of life. The Celtic strapwork below represents the rays of the Sun.

**English Oak** (right), and **Sessile Oak** (far right), are the only native British oak trees. They can be identified by differences in leaves, acorns and growth habits as shown.

# English Oak - Quercus robur

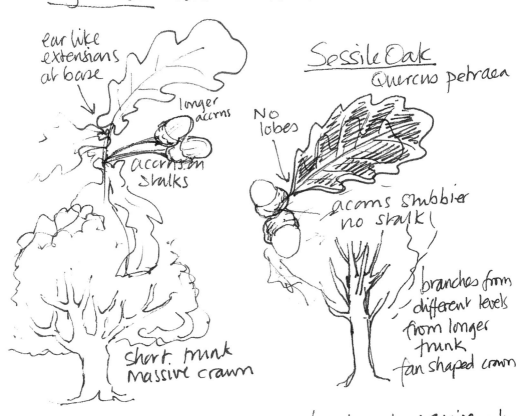

ear like extensions at base

longer acorns

acorns on stalks

## Sessile Oak
### Quercus petraea

No lobes

acorns stubbier no stalk

branches from different levels from longer trunk fan shaped crown

short trunk massive crown

Eng Oak - gr forests eg. New forest among Britain's oldest trees

dominant native oak in wetter, less fertile N & W of Britain - uplands

# The Famous Oak

To me the Oak is the most masculine, regal and English tree in the Ogham. The whole idea of "Oak" is redolent with strength, solidity and permanence, and it is no surprise that many individual oak trees have become icons of English history, recording important characters and events.

**Herne's Oak** - Windsor Great Park - felled 1796 Herne was Henry VIII's forester, and legend tells how he saved his king's life in a hunting accident. Henry's reward made Herne's rivals jealous and they contrived his downfall by seeking the help of a witch whose spell robbed him of his skills. Herne hung himself from an oak in despair. Herne the Hunter is also said to be an ancient British God, known as Cernunnos by the Celts, the lord of the wild beasts of the forest, crowned with antlers, he leads the "Wild Hunt", accompanied by his black hounds across Windsor Great Park whenever the country is threatened with calamity.

*"There is an old tale goes that Herne the Hunter,*
*Sometime a keeper here in Windsor Forest,*
*Doth all the winter time at still midnight*
*Walk round about an oak, with great ragged horns*
*And there he blasts the tree."*

Act 4, Scene 4, The Merry Wives of Windsor - William Shakespeare.
First performed April 23rd 1597 (English patron St George's day)

**Major Oak**, Sherwood Forest - the meeting place for Robin Hood's "merry men"
**Augustine's Oak**, Isle of Thanet - where King Ethelbert met Augustine 597, bringing Roman Christianity to England.
**Turpin's Oak,** Barnet - Associated with the highwayman, Dick Turpin.
**Reformation Oak,** Norwich - 1549 gathering place to repulse Royalist troops.
**Carmarthen Oak** - associated with Merlin.
**Charles' Oak**, Boscobel Wood, Shropshire - where Charles II hid from Cromwell's troops 1651 - restored to the throne 29th May 1660 (Oak Apple Day)

The legends of Herne the Hunter, Robin Hood and Merlin are all related to matters of state and the British nation, whether as warnings of strife for the country, protecting the people from oppression or as King's guide and advisor. Even the purple dye for the sovereign's robes was obtained from Oak bark!

*The Oak is called "Mighty King of the Forest", "Father of Trees".*

# The Oaken Door

*"With foot beat of the swift Oak*
*Heaven and earth rung;*
*Stout guardian of the Door,*
*His name in every tongue"*
- Taliesin, 6th century Welsh poet

It must be more than coincidence that the word "Door", the portal to inner strength and spirituality has antecedents in both Celtic language - "Duir", and Sanskrit - "Dwr". Ideas about the origins of the British people abound, but it is likely that the ancients were more sophisticated than is widely believed, and that ideas, culture and language spread all over the known world through trade by land and sea. In this way the root of the Sanskrit word Dwr, which also means Oak tree could easily have spread from the Eastern Mediterranean eastwards to India and also westwards to the Atlantic coast, then northwards to the Celtic lands along recognised ancient migration routes.

## Thunder Gods and Druids

The Oak was sacred to thunder Gods; Zeus, Jupiter and Thor (all patriarchs), whose voice is the thunder. The Blasted Oak, struck by their thunderbolts of lightning, carries their message of power. In classical Greece, the Oak Grove of Dodona was an oracle sacred to Zeus, where the priests would foretell future events by interpreting the rustling of the leaves, cooing of doves, clanking of the vessels hanging in the branches, gurgling of the sacred stream and the thunder - the voice of the Gods.

The word "Druid" derives from the Celtic "druidh," or Manx "Druaight." meaning "sage," connected with the Greek word for oak, "drus". To the Druids, Oak groves were sacred sites of worship. Mistletoe growing on oak trees was considered to be especially magical, and the berries were thought to be the semen of the God, as acorns represented the glans penis. (Acorn - "Korn", Danish = seed of the oak).

"Duir" - the 7th tree in the Ogham system covers the mid point of the year. Midsummer Baal or Bal fires often thought to be made of Oakwood, are still lit either on Midsummers Eve (June 23rd) across the beacons of Cornwall from Carn Brea to the Tamar river, or on Old Misdummers Eve (July 4th) at Whalton, Northumberland and on the Isle of Man where the day is called in Manx, Lhaa Boaldyn, "the day of Baal's fire." Baal or Bel was the Sun God.

as above
so below

Midsummer fires were usually constructed near a sacred spot, a hilltop or holy well or border place, sacred to the Celts who counted any boundary a magical place, giving entrance to and from the Otherworld. Oak wood was preferred if possible because it burns green and gives off smoke which may be used for obtaining oracular visions.

# HOLLY - TINNE

Letter - T
Number - 8
Rules - 8th July to 4th August
8th Lunar month

**Correspondences**

Element - Fire
Planet - Saturn, Mars
Gender - Masculine
Bird - Robin, Starling
Beast - Dog
Deities - Holly King, Jesus

**Interpretation**

Spear - balance and direction
Protection

holly

8th July
to
4th Aug

Tinne

8th July
to
4th August

8th July. 2·30pm, very windy, dark threatening sky, storm coming. I walked down the lane as far as where the badgers are. Here the land falls away to a deep gully, before rising again to the field beyond, this dip is almost totally concealed for most of the year by bracken and bramble thicket. On the slope opposite the road grows a huge, broad Holly tree, at least fifty feet high, with smooth pale grey bark, and many 'trunkles' with knobbly protuberances forming flaring organic shapes.

# 8th lunar month Tinne

The thin lower branches droop down to the ground and bear the most beautiful leaves, broad, full, generously spiked, but even and elegantly proportioned. Exactly what I was looking for to use as reference for a Holly King Green Man design I was working on as a Yule card!
Of all the trees there are in the wood, the Holly tree bears the crown!
I cut a branch and hurried back before the storm broke, which it soon did with a vengance! I sat indoors and watched the lightning and the rain pouring down the window, hoping the majestic Holly would fulfil its promise and protect us from storm and fire. Now is the time of the Holly King, the Oak King is spent for now.

# Holly.

# The Oak King and the Holly King

Legend tells us that the year is ruled over by two brothers, who fight for dominance every summer and winter solstice. At Yule the Oak king is triumphant, and rules until Midsummer, when at the height of his powers, he sacrifices himself, allowing the Holly king to take his turn. He too will rule until he must relinquish his power at the time of his greatest glory. And so the wheel of the year turns, held in balance, and all is as it should be.

Holly King

As the Oak King submits to the Holly King at midsummer, so the Holly King rules the waning half of the year, and takes the month after the Oak King's as his own.

*"The Holly and the Ivy, when they are both full-grown*
*Of all the trees that are in the wood,*
*the Holly bears the crown"*

The kingship of the Holly is that of the sacrificial king, the Sun King who dies and is reborn at the winter solstice. His blood is the red berries which ripen at this time and are used for Yuletide decorations as they also represent fire, warmth and light. Holly was also used for decoration at the Roman feast of Saturnalia, as it was said that the club which Saturn wielded was made of Holly. So when the date of Christmas was finalised at the same time of year, people continued to use Holly until it became part of Christmas imagery. Eventually it gave rise to the popular carol equating the red berries with the blood of Jesus, and the prickles of Holly's evergreen leaves with His crown of thorns. Holly means holy, and Tinne or Tan is the Celtic word meaning any sacred tree.

Legend tells us of the Robin, totem of the Holly, who brought the gift of fire to mankind, bringing warmth and light from the Sun, but was scorched by its heat, giving him his red breast. The Welsh name for the Robin is "bronthuddyn" which means in their tongue "singed breast", and Tinne gives us the word "Tinder" for kindling fires.

# Protection

Holly planted near a house is said to provide protection from storms, lightning and fire,. Superstition has it that no witch could cross a threshold made of Holly wood, so guaranteeing protection from curses and evil influences. However, Holly may be used in protection spells, and for magical purposes, Holly should be gathered on the solstice eve at midnight in the forest without a light, leaving an offering of a drop of your blood or red wine in exchange.

*"I am a battle waging spear,*
*I am a God who forms sacred fire for a head"*
- song of Amergin, thought to be over 3000 years old.

*"The Holly, dark green, made a resolute stand,*
*He is armed with many spear points wounding the hand"*
- Cad Goddeu, The Battle of the Trees, from the "Book of Taliesin"

Both these ancient poems, in the Druid bardic tradition, speak of Holly as a spear, and indeed, spear shafts were made of Holly wood, giving balance and direction. The prickles of the Holly leaf may also be reminiscent of the points of spears. A Holly hedge, when grown is impassable, a dense protection of prickly leaves bristling like the spears of a formation of embattled pikemen.

## Holly Decoction

Holly berries, dried and powdered, administered externally, will help to stop bleeding, but must never be used internally as they are very purgative.

Soak fresh or dried leaves in cold water for 2 hours. Bring to the boil, and simmer for ten minutes, then remove from the heat.
Allow to stand(infuse) for 10 mins. Strain, and sweeten with honey.
1 wineglass, once a day

Holly leaves are diuretic, induce sweating, and may be used to treat coughs, catarrh and bronchitis.

Flowers - May to August
Creamy white buds, snowy white flowers, 4 petals, growing in leaf axils.
4 white stamens, golden yellow pollen.

Leaves - dark shiny above, paler, smooth below.
Margins of leaf - pale creamy green.
Tips of prickles - rusty brown.

# HAZEL - COLL
Letter - C
Number - 9
Rules - 5th August to 1st September
9th Lunar month

**Correspondences**
Element - Water
Planet - Mercury
Gender - Opposite
Bird - Heron
Beast - Salmon
Deities - Connla, Fionn, Aengus

**Interpretation**
Inspiration
Wisdom, Knowledge
Fertility

# hazel

27th September. Noon, cool, overcast, autumnal.
The Hazel I planted beside my studio window is now
ten feet tall and in summertime gives a dappled shade
of liquid greens. Watching over my creative processes,
I often gaze at it when in need of inspiration.
The nuts have all gone now, squirrel food! The sholls
lie in halves on the ground and crackle underfoot.
Next years catkins are already almost an inch long,
pale green and tight. The round serrated, rough, hairy
leaves are starting to change to autumn colours,
yellowing, russet tipped. The hairy pinkish stems
growing from leaf axils bear pale buds, though the
terminal buds on main shoots are red. The many
rods, growing from ground level have smooth bark,
reddish brown and shiny. The straightest one I have
earmarked as a walking stick, and having trimmed
off the side shoots, I will wait until it is thick
enough before cutting and carving it for my old age.

**5th Aug
to
1st Sept**

The tree will know when it will be needed!
Funny, the books say this is a feminine tree,
but this one feels most definitely male.
A guardian, standing at the gateway, cool, solid
rough, with an aura that feels like the knowledge
of being. Just **IS**. Mystery, but not mysterious,
Just **IS**, but different. Permanence, almost
Indifference.

  Post Script —
I now believe that Coll is 'other' — opposite to
the observer, so appears to be masculine to me
because I am female. I have learned not to take
received wisdom as indisputable. Test it for
yourself and don't let anyone tell you
what to think.

**Coll**

# Inspiration

The Hazel tree growing outside my studio window provides me with an unfailing source of inspiration as I gaze at its broad shade in summer and the delicate catkins in winter. But this is not the only Hazel tree to serve as such, there are ancient stories . . .

In Irish legend, Connla's well was overhung by nine Hazel trees which contained all the knowledge of the arts and sciences. The nuts which hung from the trees imparted that wisdom to those who ate them. When the Hazelnuts dropped into the well, they were eaten by the salmon living there, who developed a spot on his skin for each of the nine nuts as a symbol of this knowledge. Fionn, the son of the chief Druid's daughter, cooked the salmon for the chief Druid to eat, but he was forbidden to taste it, though when he burnt his thumb on the hot fish, he sucked it to ease the pain, and gained the wisdom by accident.

This tale of knowledge, unintentionally stolen from the master by a novice, has echoes in many mythologies - the Welsh story of Gwion, who stirred the cauldron of Ceridwen, for a year and a day, to brew magical knowledge destined for her ill favoured son Afagddu, when three splashes burnt his thumb; he also sucked it, and realising he had gained the wisdom, he fled with Ceridwen pursuing, changing shape continuously, into a hare and hound, fish and otter, bird and hawk, until as a grain of corn Ceridwen the hen ate him. Soon Ceridwen magically bore a beautiful son but knowing it was Gwion cast him adrift on the river. Stuck in a salmon weir he was found by a king's son, who named him Taliesin - shining golden brow - later the great bard and seer.

The three drops of inspiration have now been adopted as the badge of many modern Druids, and Druid heralds carry a white hazel wand as a symbol of their authority. Aengus, the Irish God of love, also carried a hazel wand.

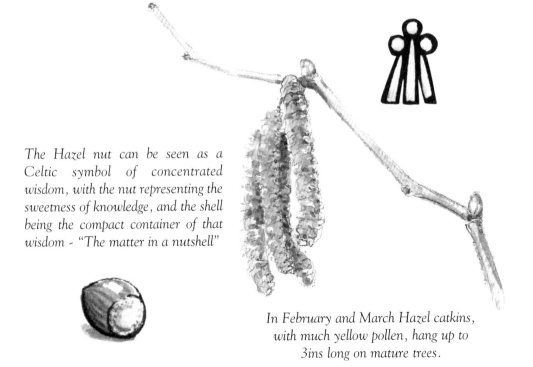

*The Hazel nut can be seen as a Celtic symbol of concentrated wisdom, with the nut representing the sweetness of knowledge, and the shell being the compact container of that wisdom - "The matter in a nutshell"*

*In February and March Hazel catkins, with much yellow pollen, hang up to 3ins long on mature trees.*

# Dowsing, Charms and Other Uses

Hazel dowsing rods have long been used to locate underground water. Cut a length of branch with a fork in it, so that the "handles" are about a foot long, and they meet together with another six inches pointing forwards. Holding the handles pulled slightly apart, so that there is a slight tension to them, and with arms stretched forwards a little, walk slowly over the ground to be dowsed. The dowsing rod will twitch downwards, attracted to the water as you pass above a subterranean water course or spring.

In times when houses were mostly constructed from wood and other combustible materials, house fires were a constant danger, and charms to protect the home were many. Three pieces of hazel wood driven into the walls of a house would protect from fire, or an equal armed Hazel twig cross, bound with red thread to preserve good luck. But if a fire should start, you could always use a Hazel dowsing rod to locate the water to put out the flames!

**Wood -** Hazel is often coppiced for flexible rods, which can be used as wattle for walls, hurdles and fences, or woven into baskets and bentwood furniture.

Hazel may be grown as a hedge, as its branching growth from ground level creates a dense barrier. Hazel rods are also woven through thorn trees in some styles of hedge-laying.

**True Love and Fertility -** Divination at Halloween; place hazel nuts, each named for a lover, together in the fire, as the nuts are roasted, if they spit or jump it signifies there is no love there, but if they burn quietly together, the love between you is true.

*July -*
*Cobnuts*
*Cob = Coll?*

## Harvest cakes
6 oz ground hazel nuts
half a cup of honey
1oz flour
1 beaten egg
Juice and grated peel of one lemon
Blend honey and nuts, add flour and peel.
Mix lemon juice and egg and add to nut mixture.
Put small amounts on to a baking sheet and cook at
350 F, 170 C for 20 mins.

### To treat a cold
*Ground hazel nuts mixed with honey and water or mead for coughs and colds. Add pepper to draw mucus from sinuses.*

# THE NUTTING GIRL

O come all you jovial fellows, listen to my song,
It is a little ditty and it won't detain you long.
It's of a fair young damsel, she lived down in Kent,
Arose one summers morning and she a-nutting went.

With my fal-lal, to me ral tal-lal, whack for the dear ol' day,
And what few nuts that poor girl had she threw them all away.

'Twas of a brisk young farmer, ploughing of his land,
He called unto his horses to bid them gently stand.
As he sat down upon his plough for a song to sing,
His voice was so melodious, it made the valleys ring.

'Twas of this brisk young damsel, nutting in the wood,
his voice was so melodious it charmed her as she stood,
she had no longer power in the lonely wood to stay,
and what few nuts she had, poor girl, she threw them all away.

She came up to young Johnny as he sat on his plough,
Says she "young man I really feel I cannot tell you how"
So he took her to some shady broom, there he laid her down,
Says she "young man I think I feel the world go round and round"

So come all you local women that listen to my song,
If you should a-nutting go, don't stay out too long
For if you should stay too long to hear that ploughboy sing
You might have a young farmer to nurse up in the spring.

- traditional

Going Nutting, while being a normal occupation of foraging for food, also provided an opportunity for young people going into the woods to engage in secret trysts, and became connected with fertility, as in the traditional song of the Nutting Girl, which was the first song I ever sang in public in a folk club, aged about fifteen.

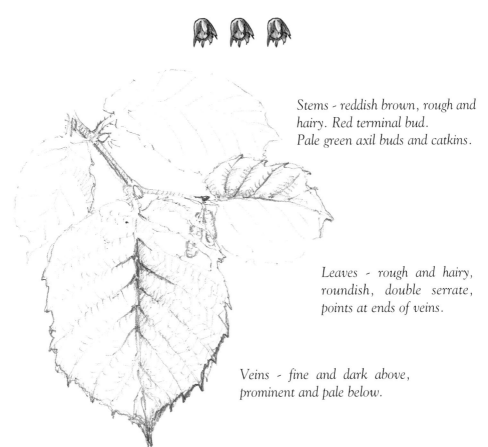

*Stems - reddish brown, rough and hairy. Red terminal bud. Pale green axil buds and catkins.*

*Leaves - rough and hairy, roundish, double serrate, points at ends of veins.*

*Veins - fine and dark above, prominent and pale below.*

# APPLE - QUERT

Letter - Q
Number - 10
Rules - The light half of the year
from Mayday to Halloween

## Correspondences

Element - Water
Cardinal point - West
Time - Sunset
Metal - Gold
Planet - Venus
Gender - Feminine
Bird - Wren
Beast - Serpent
Deities - Aphrodite, Eve, the Hesperides

## Interpretation

Healing, Wholeness
Immortality, the magical Isle in the West
Tree of Knowledge
Token of love, respect & worth
Responsibility for the consequences of ones own actions

**Apple**

Rules the light half of the year. Mayday to Halloween

**Quert**

# APPLE

17th August. It's the middle of the harvest, most fields are cut, some are already ploughed. Mid morning, sunny, warm, humid, some cloud, showery. New Moon. The day after the Boscastle flood when storm water crashed through the town leaving devastation in it's wake.

I walked down the lane towards the pond where a huge old ancient mother apple tree grows, as high as a house, amazingly fertile, protective and nurturing. Drooping boughs burdened with beautiful abundance. Mountains of apples, just flushing red. But beneath her skirts was a

# Quert

Rules the light half of the year Mayday — Halloween

whole secret world of deep green shadowy blacks - cool, dark dampness, soft, wet, quiet but for the lazy buzz of intoxicated insects gorging on fallen apples. Sensuous, fragrant, inviting. Fruits of all sorts coming — nuts, sloes, blackberries. A time of plenty is here. When I finally dragged myself away and started home, I watched a family of wrens having 'Nursery flying lessons' in the trees around the pond, 8 or 9 babies flying in line behind their mother — a wren train! As I walked back I could hear a gentle pattering sound approaching — strange, what's that? Then I laughed as the softest, warmest shower of rain washed over me!

# Wassailing

*from old English "Waes Hael"- be whole, or good health.*

An ancient custom which takes place around the turn of the year. There are two forms of wassailing -

1) House visiting, providing entertainment in the form of singing, mumming etc. for a reward of food and drink or money. Probably the forerunner of carolling at Christmas.

2) Wassailing apple orchards (mainly in Herefordshire and the West Country) to encourage a good crop for the next year. In recent years there has been a

tremendous resurgence of interest in wassailing, and many commercial apple growers have revived the custom in their own orchards, to great effect! Usually this is done on old twelfth night- 17th January.

We always bless the apple trees in our garden, ever since we planted them soon after moving here, combining a wassailing party with a belated house warming. All our friends assembled and we wassailed every tree in sight (except the leylandii)!

This year we were invited to the Whimple Wassail in Devon, where the Whiteways Cyder Co. once flourished. Everyone met in the pub just after dark, some were dressed in old fashioned farmers' smocks, many with hats decorated with Ivy, some carrying fiddles, melodeons or drums, a few had shotguns, and everyone clutched a pot or pan, mug or tankard.

Festivities commenced with a quick run through of the processional tune for the musicians, the first time it had been played since last year, and a chorus of the wassailing song for those who were a bit "rusty". Then all outside to get on with the serious business - with a rousing rendition of the song led by Jim Causley with his accordion and everyone trying to follow the words on their song sheets by the light of flaming torches. In the garden next to the pub, grows one of the few remaining famous "Whimple Wonder" apple trees. The wassail queen and princess, two young girls from the village, chanted the blessing under the tree-

"Old apple tree we wassail thee and hoping thou wilt bear
Hatfuls, capfuls, three bushel bagfuls, and little heaps under the stairs"

- and placed toast soaked in spiced cider in the branches to feed the birds - and the spirits of the trees. "Hip, hip- hooray" everyone shouted, making as much noise as they can, bashing pots and tins, beating drums. Then the shotguns are fired over the tree! The deafening noise is to frighten away the evil spirits who might be lurking to cause mischief and to blight the crop. As if by magic, a steaming bucket of hot spiced cider appears, and the crowd surges forward to scoop it up in their mugs, cups and tankards. Mmmm…!

When everyone has partaken of the communal drink, the party processes to the next stopping place. In the middle of the village we paused while the chap from the history society told us stories of local people and events - the folklore of tomorrow. Then the band played the processional tune and the drums sounded a steady, hypnotic heartbeat as we marched, hundreds strong, through the dark streets of the village to the first of the two orchards to be wassailed that night.

The atmosphere is hard to describe. A Wassailing can be a fun evening out with friends in a muddy orchard (wear your wellies!), laughing and singing and having a great time, or it can be a moving and spiritual experience, as you connect with the earth and the spirits of the apple trees to seek a blessing for the good of the local people. The experience of walking to the beat of drums and music is in itself uplifting. The darkness adds mystery and a slight feeling of unease, but also releases inhibitions as you are almost totally disguised in the gloom and can feel so much closer to the otherworld.

It is undoubtedly brilliant social cement, bringing together the whole community for the purpose of a bit of sympathetic magic, encouraging the production of the raw materials for making next year's cider - it does inevitably end up in the pub (or in this case the cricket club bar)!

## Wassail Recipe

1ltr Dry cider, 2 tablespoons brown sugar, 1 stick cinnamon
12 cloves, 3 slices fresh ginger, Slices of apple

Place all ingredients in a saucepan and heat gently, do not boil as this will evaporate the alcohol! Keep the wassail just below boiling point for 20mins to develop the flavour. Top up the saucepan with more cider, adding sugar and spices as required. Serve poured through a sieve to remove spices, in a large three handled Wassail bowl, passed from hand to hand around the assembled company. Or served in a large pan into which cups may be dipped
- enjoy! Waes hael!

# Golden Apples

Once again there are tales from parallel mythologies, this time Greek and Norse, telling of golden apples which impart youth, vigour and immortality to the Gods who must eat them to retain their powers. In fact the medicinal qualities of apples are well documented. In addition to their vitamin and fibre content, apples are a tonic, blood cleanser and alleviate the symptoms of rheumatism, so the Gods do well to eat them!

The golden apple tree was tended by Idun of the Vanir in the Northern tradition; and in Greece, by the Hesperides, the three daughters of Hesperus, the evening star, and Atlas who supported the world on his shoulders. This tree grew in a garden on a magical island west of the setting sun, and was guarded by Ladon the great serpent, slain by Heracles whilst stealing the apples as one of his twelve labours.

Serpents shed their skin as they grow and appear to be reborn anew, as the serpent who eats his own tail in a never ending circle, symbolises immortality, and the eternal cycles of life.

I incorporated many of these ideas into a "Golden Apples" design, with the serpent Ladon becoming the symbol of infinity, coiling around the apple tree in a figure of eight, eternally guarding the innocence of the Hesperides, as they joyfully dance under the magical fruit.

Greek legend tells of the golden apple of discord, inscribed "for the fairest" and tossed into the midst of the assembled goddesses. Hera, Athene and Aphrodite all claimed the apple and Paris, prince of Troy, had to judge between them. Aphrodite promised him the most beautiful woman alive if he chose her, but when Paris claimed Helen as his reward, her abduction from her husband started the ill fated Trojan Wars.

The apple tree and the serpent appear again in the Jewish tale of the Garden of Eden, when Adam and Eve eat of the fruit of the tree of knowledge and are turned out of the garden.

So what the apple teaches is not always benign, as sometimes the consequences can be unforeseen and not entirely pleasant. As "The Apple of my eye" may be an endearment and token of favour, so "An apple for the teacher", though well worth a try for a better mark, might just get you a reputation as "teacher's pet"!

Cut an apple in half crossways, to reveal a five pointed star, the pentagram, representing the elements air, fire, water, earth and spirit; magical protection; the five senses; and the figure of mankind.

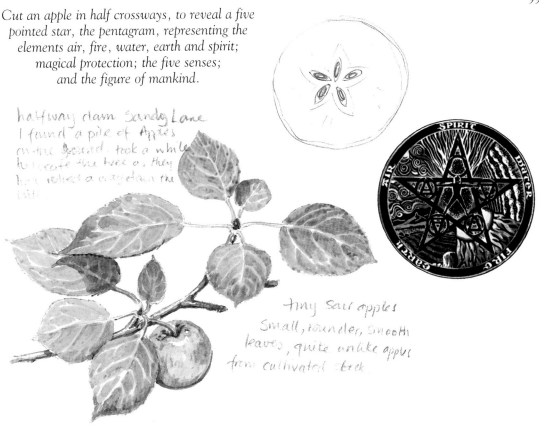

hallway dawn Sandy Lane
I found a pile of Apples
on the beward. took a while
to locate the tree as they
had rolled a way down the
hill.

tiny sour apples
Small, rounder, smooth
leaves, quite unlike apples
from cultivated stock.

**Crab Apple** trees are native British trees and the ancestral stock from which cultivated apples were developed.

To me, the apple can be seen as a symbol of the sun; when yellow it represents the midday sun high in the sky, but as it ripens to red it becomes the glorious colour of the setting sun sinking over the horizon in the west.

Apple = Sun

Yellow apple    red apple = sunset (west)

# BRAMBLE - MUIN

Letter - M
Number - 11
Rules - 2nd September to 29th September
10th lunar month

## Correspondences

Element - Water
Planet - Venus
Gender - Feminine
Bird - Titmouse (blue tit)
Deities - Feare folk (fairies), Triple Goddess
Dionysus, Bacchus - wine Gods

## Interpretation

Linking, Connections
Intoxication

Bramble

2ⁿᵈ Sept
to
29ᵗʰ Sept

Muin

BRamble

September —
When we first moved to
Southey Green — the very first
Autumn, in September, I was
seized by a sort of obsession,
an uncontrollable need to gather
and preserve all the fruit that
burdened the hedgerows. I made
blackberry jam, elderberry cough
mixture, blackberry and apple pies
and crumbles, stewed fruit, sloe gin...
it nearly killed me! I was out
every evening after work
in the lane collecting, then
in the kitchen half the
night stewing, pickling
and bottling.
I couldn't help myself —

# muin

I had been taken over by some sort of primeval survival instinct. As if my life depended on it, with the lean months of winter fast approaching. The next autumn, even though I'd given away loads of home-made pots of this and that, the cupboards were still half full of it. I'm a bit more careful now as to what and how much I preserve. But it's good to know that I am still in touch with the passage of the seasons.

# Muin - Vine or Bramble?

Some sources state that in the original Ogham system Muin is Vine. This is puzzling as I always understood from my school history lessons that vines were introduced by the Romans, who also, according to their own historians, wiped out the Druids, shortly after they (the Romans) arrived here. If the Druids developed the Ogham, then the whole system must have grown up, evolved and been wiped out in just a few years.

There are several possible alternative explanations. Either vines had come to Britain considerably earlier, brought by traders and travellers from Europe. Or could the Ogham system have developed with the Celtic peoples as they migrated northwards from the Mediterranean, via the Iberian Peninsula, and so have been already in existence before the Celts reached Britain. Coming from Gaul or the Iberian Peninsula, both vine-growing areas, the association would be perfectly natural. Whatever the truth of the matter, vines require warmth and sunshine and, even though it is recorded that the climate was warmer during Roman times than it is now, in Britain vines only grow in certain mild sheltered places, and are not regarded as native. So vine was replaced by Bramble, which has many of the same properties and habit, scrambling and climbing, and producing fruit which makes good wine. Bramble is a native plant, is far tougher and can easily withstand the British climate, growing freely (some would say a bit too freely!)just about everywhere.  Here, in this place, the only vine that used to grow (in Old Bob's hedge) has withered and diminished. So as Bramble is extremely plentiful, I included it as being most appropriate.

# Making Connections

When I was at school, studying for 'O'levels, one way I used to memorise a chunk of text was by setting it to the tune of a pop song. This proved most successful in the case of Biology, when I had to learn about Bramble's vegetative reproduction. Set to the tune of Simon and Garfunkle's "Homeward Bound", I can still remember, word perfect, to this day:

*"The Bramble produces woody branches that bend over and touch the ground (mm-mm), and develop swollen tips from which leaves and adventitious roots arise, new shoots grow out from among the leaves and become independent plants. This is an example of vegetative or asexual reproduction"*

As the Bramble continues to throw out arching stems that root and start new growth, it gradually develops into a thicket, a web; tough, thorny and binding.

With the help of Bramble wine, altered states of consciousness may have given rise to the belief that the fruit of the Bramble, Blackberries, are the food of the faere folk, and Bramble thickets guard fairy mounds. Perhaps the analogy of a door to the otherworld has been used to remind us of this, as when in a state of intoxication, with inhibitions reduced and receptiveness to spiritual consciousness enhanced, the otherworld is more easily accessible.

As Bramble clambers through hedgerows linking trees shrubs and bushes together with long thorny braids, so knowledge is linked and connections made to make sense of disjointed scraps of information. Bramble wine can be very strong and heady, intoxicating. In the same way, ideas can be very exciting when chanced upon by linking disparate bits of knowledge, enthusing, intoxicating ideas inspiring intellectual activity and visionary thought.

As Blackberries ripen, the colours
represent aspects of the Triple Goddess -
Green - maiden
Red - mother
Black - crone

Bramble leaves - usually
3 or 5 leaflets, sometimes
an intermediate form with
"fused" double leaflets occurs.

Superstition says that the Devil spits on the Blackberries,
on 30th September, the day after the end of Bramble's
month, and they must not be eaten after that date.

## Blackberry Jam

2 lb Blackberries
2 lb Sugar

Pick over the blackberries to remove stalks etc. and rinse well. Place in a large saucepan with 2 tablespoons water, and bring to the boil. Simmer for 5 mins, until the fruit is cooked and softened. Add sugar, bring to a rolling boil. Boil for 8 - 10 mins. Test for setting by placing a teaspoonful on a cold saucer, push your finger through the cooled jam, if it wrinkles it's ready. Pour into hot, sterilised jars and seal.

## Blackberry & Apple Crumble

2 handfulls ripe Blackberries, washed
1 large or 2 small Bramley apples, peeled & sliced
6 oz plain flour (I use Doves farm gluten free)
5 oz butter
5 oz sugar

Put blackberries & apples in an oven proof dish. Rub the butter into the flour until it resembles breadcrumbs, and add the sugar. Sprinkle the crumble over the fruit. Bake in a preheated oven, 170 C, 325F, Gas Mk 3 for 45 mins. Serve with evaporated milk or vanilla ice cream.

## Bramble leaf tea

Urinary tonic or as a mouthwash or gargle also for blackheads and acne
1 oz dried leaves
1 pt water
Bring to the boil and simmer for five minutes. Remove from heat, strain.
Take 3 – 4 times a day.

# IVY - GORT

Letter G
Number - 12
Rules - 30th September to 27th October
11th lunar month

**Correspondences**
Element - Water
Planet - Saturn
Gender - Feminine
Bird - Swan
Deities - Saturn, Dionysus, Corn God

**Interpretation**
Preservation
Perseverance
Transformation through Persistence

Ivy

30th Sept
to
27th Oct

GORT

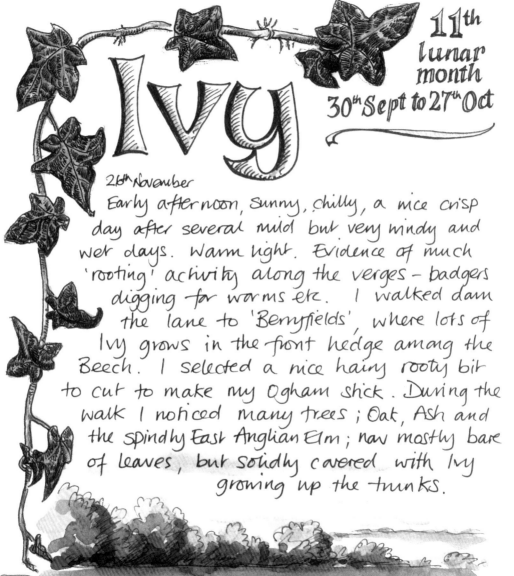

# Ivy

**11th lunar month**
**30th Sept to 27th Oct**

26th November

Early afternoon, sunny, chilly, a nice crisp day after several mild but very windy and wet days. Warm light. Evidence of much 'rooting' activity along the verges – badgers digging for worms etc. I walked down the lane to 'Berryfields', where lots of Ivy grows in the front hedge among the Beech. I selected a nice hairy rooty bit to cut to make my Ogham stick. During the walk I noticed many trees; Oak, Ash and the spindly East Anglian Elm; now mostly bare of leaves, but solidly covered with Ivy growing up the trunks.

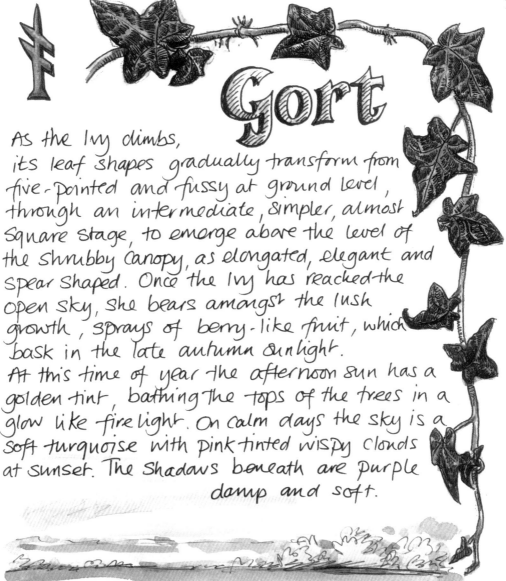

# Gort

As the Ivy climbs, its leaf shapes gradually transform from five-pointed and fussy at ground level, through an intermediate, simpler, almost square stage, to emerge above the level of the shrubby canopy, as elongated, elegant and spear shaped. Once the Ivy has reached the open sky, she bears amongst the lush growth, sprays of berry-like fruit, which bask in the late autumn sunlight.

At this time of year the afternoon sun has a golden tint, bathing the tops of the trees in a glow like fire light. On calm days the sky is a soft turquoise with pink tinted wispy clouds at sunset. The shadows beneath are purple damp and soft.

# The Ivy Girl & the Wren House

At the end of the harvest the last sheaf of corn may be bound round with Ivy, the "Ivy Girl". The sheaf of corn represents fertility and the food of the people, while the evergreen Ivy represents the preserving force, the life giving spirit, just as Ivy provides shelter for wildlife in winter, preserving life when most trees and hedges are bare.

The Roman feast of Saturnalia was held at midwinter, and Saturn's Holly club was crowned with Ivy, forming a nest for Saturn's sacred bird, the Wren, as a house to preserve the spirit of life during the darkness of winter, ready for rebirth with the coming year.

The image of the club of Saturn with its Ivy Wren house is preserved in customs still celebrated in parts of Britain and Ireland. On 26th December, St Stephen's Day, Wren hunting ceremonies take place in Dublin and in Dingle, Co. Kerry, on the west coast of Ireland, also in the Isle of Man. 'The King', an old song from Pembrokeshire tells of hunting the Wren.

# The Cutty Wren

The Wren ceremony I attend most years is "The Cutty Wren" in Middleton, Suffolk, also on St. Stephen's day, late in the evening when it is quite dark. The company assembles at the village hall and processes along the main street to The Bell public house at the other end of the village, led by a broom-man sweeping the path to clear the way, and the Cutty Wren (cutty means small), housed in a globe of Ivy on top of a tall pole decorated with ribbons, attended by the Old Glory Molly dancers, all male, who will dance outside the pub before story telling and singing inside. The musicians who play for the dancing are all female, dressed in black and their hats are trimmed with masses of Ivy. The procession is lit by flaming torches and takes place in silence apart from the slow beat of one drum, giving the sombreness of a funeral to the proceedings. This ceremony was based closely on a custom that took place annually in Middleton until the end of the 19th century, and was revived in 1994 by Old Glory and Pete Jennings.

# Transformation

Some interpret Ivy as binding, restricting, holding down, limiting; as ivy binds trees and eventually suffocates, so personal desires are subjugated by responsibilities to others; striving in the face of criticism or antagonism; hidden obstacles.

BUT - are you the tree or the Ivy? Ivy overcomes enormous obstacles, climbs huge trees and in the process transforms itself. At ground level, Ivy bears dark, five pointed, complicated leaves, and is searching for the light; this represents the tangled and difficult lives we lead when we can only see the mundane world around us. As Ivy climbs the heights of the host tree, it transforms itself, with brighter, simplified leaves, and bears fruit. This transformation is the reward for seeking and perseverance, it takes courage to fight our way through the distractions of our lives, and try to keep focused on what is really important, to learn the lessons we are here to learn.

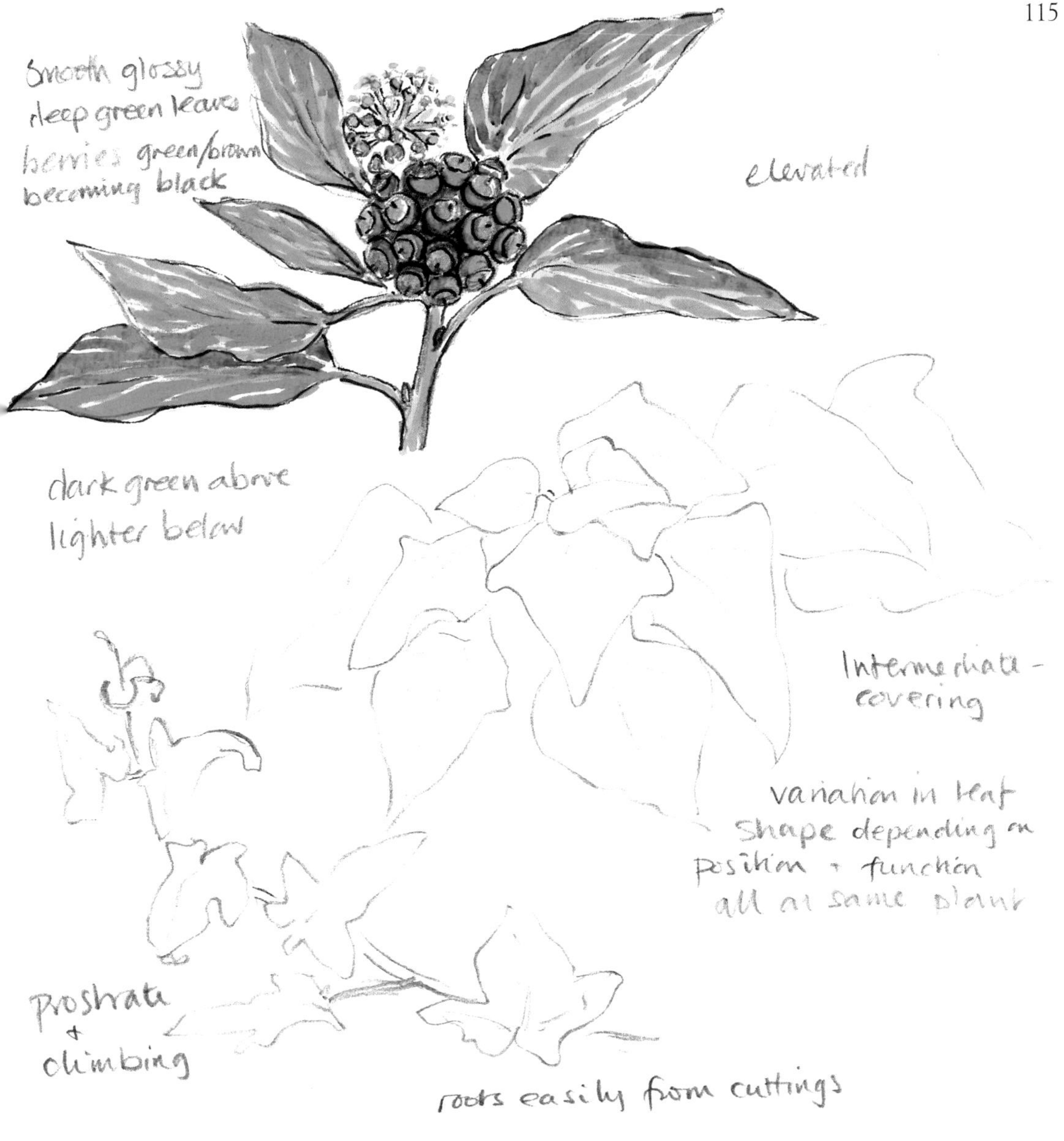

Smooth glossy
deep green leaves
berries green/brown
becoming black

elevated

dark green above
lighter below

Intermediate -
covering

variation in leaf
shape depending on
position + function
all on same plant

prostrate
+
climbing

roots easily from cuttings

# WHEATSTRAW - NGETAL

Letter - Ng
Number - 13
Rules - 28th October to 24th November
12th lunar month

**Correspondences**

Element - Fire
Planet - Sun
Gender - Masculine
Bird - Goose
Deities - Corn god, John Barleycorn

**Interpretation**

Symbol of Power
Sovereignty, Kingship
The source of life giving sustenance

Wheatstraw

28th Oct
to
24th Nov

Ngetal

# WHEAT

In the early days, when I set out to study the Ogham, I realised that there were choices to be made. There are several slightly different versions of the system, as both time and geography have caused variations to occur. Although the alternatives mostly have similar interpretations, there have been good historical reasons for the changes. Gradually I developed two methods to help me decide which of the alternatives is most appropriate for me.

I started by using Robert Graves "The White Goddess" as my main source book.

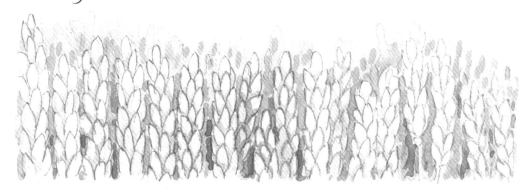

# STRAW

Ngetal

He always had an opinion as to which of the alternatives was most "correct", but although the breadth of his knowledge of mythology was breathtaking, it gradually dawned on me that he was baffling me with bullshit. But did he actually prove his case? – So – Reed or wheat straw? I decided to consult the trees (well, plants anyway) in my own place –the spirits I live among– and they soon put me right! And anyway, there's a dirty great cornfield right outside my front door, and hardly a reed for miles!

# The King and Harvest Customs

I f the most basic of all human needs are food, drink and shelter, there are few sources of the requirements of these more fundamental than corn, in Europe either wheat or barley. Bread to eat, beer to drink and straw for thatching, brick making and bedding - all have been essential for people's survival in these islands for many centuries.

In the most ancient hunter/gatherer, nomadic and fisher societies, Reed was often a symbol of power. Although society had begun its long transition to settled patterns of farming by the time of the Egyptian Pharaohs, the sceptre, signifying supreme authority, was still fashioned in the shape of a reed. The symbol persisted for a further thousand years. During his trial, a reed was mockingly placed in Jesus' hands and he was dressed in scarlet, the garb of a king, perhaps a sacrificial King.

As pastoral, settled, agricultural society superseded previous ways in more fertile lands, so wheat was adopted as the symbol of sovereignty, and the new order began to revolve around the annual cycle

Wheatstraw
Strawdollies
cornjdollies
Crowning corn God
Sacrifice of corn God
at harvest
Poppies = blood of
Sacrificial offering
ear of corn = regal
sceptre

Cornucopia —
bounty of harvest
life for the people
given by sacrifice
of the
corn
God

wheat straw & Reed
symbolic of kingship
feeding responsibility
sovereignty

of its ploughing, sowing and harvesting. So it is not surprising that this cycle has been invested with much ceremony and ritual, as people's lives were bound up with the success of the harvest as a matter, quite literally, of life and death.

Many ancient harvest customs still exist as echoes from the past. The last sheaf to be cut is thought to house the spirit of the corn, and often given a ceremonial name. This has been recorded in Devon (Crying the Neck and the Kirn Babby), Hertfordshire (the Mare), Shropshire (the old Hare), Hampshire (Kern Baby) and the Highlands of Scotland (A Mhaighdean, or Maiden). This sacred load is often accompanied with rituals for its cutting and transporting, to preserve the corn spirit, later degenerating into merely "good luck", for the benefit of the community.

Often a Corn Dolly was made from the choicest corn, crafted in the shape of a female figure or a receptacle in which the spirit of the harvest was said to reside. These dollies were often decorated with flowers, treated with great reverence, and carried from the field on top of the last cartload, being preserved in a place of honour until either the next harvest, or, in some places, ploughed into the land on the following Plough Monday in order to maintain fertility.

If the harvest was good it would be a time of great rejoicing and though the work was hard and long, as shearing by hand could take weeks. The gangs of men who cut the corn and the women, who followed behind tying the sheaves and tending the men, would sing and banter to encourage each other and keep spirits up. With the precious crop safely stowed in the barns, all who had contributed to the work would be rewarded with a great feast, provided by the farmer, and singing, dancing and jollity would last well into the night.

# JOHN BARLEYCORN

There were three men came from the west
Their fortune for to try,
And these three men made a solemn vow
John Barleycorn should die.

They ploughed him in three furrows deep,
Threw sods upon his head,
Then these three men made a solemn vow
John Barleycorn was dead.

They let him lie for a very long time,
Till the rain from heaven did fall,
Then little Sir John raised up his head
And he did amaze them all.

They let him lie till midsummer's day,
Till he looked both pale and wan,
Then little Sir John grew a long beard
And so became a man.

Then they hired men with scythes so sharp
To cut him off at the knee,
And they rolled him and bound him
  round the waist,
Served him most barbarously.

Then they hired men with sharp pitchforks
To pierce him to the heart,
But the loader served him worse than that,
For he bound him to the cart.

Then they wheeled him round and round
  the field
Till they came unto a barn,
And there they made a solemn vow
On poor John Barleycorn.

Then they hired men with crab tree sticks
To cut him skin from bone,
But the miller served him worse than that
For he ground him between two stones.

There's little Sir John in the nut brown bowl
And Brandy in the glass,
But little Sir John in the nut brown bowl
Proved the stronger man at last.

For the huntsman, he can't hunt the fox
Nor loudly blow the horn,
And the tinker can't mend his kettles and pots
Without a little Barleycorn.

- traditional

# Plough Monday

*Speed the Plough*

The Monday after twelfth night is traditionally the day on which ploughing was resumed after Christmas, when the land had been frozen and no work could be done. But before ploughing could recommence, a day of merrymaking was celebrated, in different ways all over Eastern England from Yorkshire to East Anglia. Plough boys would take out entertainment, begging for "Largesse" to tide them over, since their enforced break with no wages. In East Anglia, the "Molly Gangs" or "Plough Witches" would go out into the villages,

disguised with blackened faces and their clothes decked with coloured ribbons, to dance for the amusement of the "well to do", and to scrounge whatever food or money they could. If nothing was given, the plough they carried with them would be used to rake a furrow through the lawn of the uncharitable! Hence the disguise, if they had been recognised they would probably have lost their jobs!

Strangely, "blacking up" is a remarkably good disguise. I would not have believed how good, had I not encountered several friends, dancing with a team of Molly dancers, in a shopping centre several years ago, with faces totally blacked with stage make-up, and I have to admit I found it impossible to recognise most of them!

125

Molly dancing is a bit like country dancing, mostly done by men (though not always) in hob-nailed boots, often with a "Lord and Lady" to lead the set. It still goes on; in fact it is undergoing a huge revival at present, there are gangs who wear the traditional Victorian workmen's garb, but increasingly new teams are going in for more spectacular kit; psychedelic colours or striking black and white, and they even have their own festival -"Whittlesey Straw Bear" in the Fens every January. On the Saturday, the "Bear", a man dressed in a suit of straw, the manifestation of the agricultural spirit of the Fenland area, with Keeper and entourage, parades around the town, presiding over a street dance convention, mainly the Molly Dancers of East Anglia. Then on Sunday, the Bear leads a final procession to his ceremonial burning - releasing the spirit of the Old Year into the New.

I go out with Good Easter Molly Gang on Plough Monday, and play a large, rope-tensioned drum, touring the rural pubs of Essex, usually taking in a primary school in the morning to dance for the children, and ending up with a feast.

What a way to encourage the fertility of the land every year!

*far left - Good Easter Molly    above - Pig Dyke Molly*

# BLACKTHORN - STRAIF

Letter - Ss
Number - 14
Rules - the dark half of the year
from Halloween to Mayday

## Correspondences

Element - Earth
Planet - Saturn
Gender - Feminine
Bird - Thrush
Deities - Crone, Faere folk

## Interpretation

Strife, Slay, Defend
Secrets, Magic

Blackthorn

Rules the dark
half of the
year
halloween to
Mayday

Shillelagh

Straif

# BLACKTHORN

17th April the next year. Early evening, a warm sunny day. Spring is truly here. Yesterday I saw the first swallow, and Blackthorn is in full blossom all along the lane.

Opposite Hill Farm is an area that was once common land, but in recent years has become overgrown with Blackthorn, spreading by means of underground roots and suckers, to form an incredibly dense thicket, providing cover for hundreds of rabbits.

The blossom here is stunning!

I walked towards the plantation, signs of spring all around me, and thought about the long dark months and bitter cold of winter. I remember as a child waking up in the mornings, seeing ice making ferny patterns on the inside of my window, pulling my clothes into the bed to warm them up and getting dressed under the blankets – and that was in a 3-bedroom semi with a fire! How much harder it must have been for people in the times the Ogham was made? The Blackthorn blossom that's all around me today must have been a very welcome sight indeed for them, as it meant "We did it, we survived!" Returning through the harefield and along the path towards the Black Barn, I cut a sprig of Blackthorn to draw, with flowers and leaf buds just starting to open. Only just in time, but it is still the time of Blackthorn – just!

Rules the Dark half
of the Year
Halloween to Mayday

Straif

# The Dark Half of the Year

Blackthorn, whose wood is dense and strong, is used for clubs and weapons, walking sticks and staffs. The famous Irish "shillelagh" is a blackthorn walking stick, doubling as a club at need. Blackthorn rules the dark half of the year, and also represents the dark side of our imaginations. During the darkness of winter time, when the shadows may hide all manner of menacing and frightening threats, bent and wizened with age, Blackthorn the "increaser of secrets" is immensely strong in spirit, and defiant in the face of adversity. The essence of Blackthorn is support and defence, a crutch and a cudgel, but it must be wielded with compassion and wisdom or it may destroy the user. The long sharp thorns of the Blackthorn were used to prick wax poppets (dolls fashioned in the likeness of the subject of a curse), but beware - the law of threefold return, or karma, will ensure that what goes around, comes around!

# Sloe Stones and Feare Folk

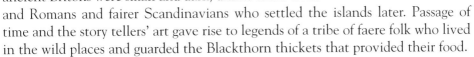

The vast number of Sloe stones found in excavations of some Neolithic sites shows that Sloes, the bitter fruit of the Blackthorn, were eaten by ancient British people over a wide area. Archaeology suggests that some ancient Britons were small and dark, unlike taller Celts and Romans and fairer Scandinavians who settled the islands later. Passage of time and the story tellers' art gave rise to legends of a tribe of faere folk who lived in the wild places and guarded the Blackthorn thickets that provided their food.

Blackthorn rules the dark half of the year as it provides the strength of spirit needed to survive the winter months, together with its gifts of food (sloes) and warming drink (sloe gin) needed for sustenance, and protection from cold weather and danger (wood to burn, thorn thickets and weapons).

Blackthorn comes into its own with the winter, when the sloes are plentiful, though they are far too sour to eat by modern tastes, they make a wonderful warming Yuletide drink, and the twigs can be used to make seasonal decorations that look great and cost nothing but a few scratches!

# Sloe Gin

Fresh picked Sloes, washed
2 - 3 heaped tablespoons sugar
Bottle of Gin

In late September or October, when they are fully ripe, pick your Sloes. If there has been a frost, all the better, if not, you can put your sloes in the freezer for a few days to break down the cellular structure a bit, and split the tough skins. Prick them all over with a pin (I use two sharp forks – it's much quicker!), and pack them into wide topped, water tight jars – about half full. Then add sugar, to taste. 2-3 tbsp for a 1 litre jar. Top up with Gin, leaving a little gap at the top. Shake the jar every day to thoroughly blend all the ingredients and develop the flavour. By Yuletide it will be a rich tawny colour ready to decant and drink, but if you can bear to leave some to mature longer, it improves with keeping.

# Yuletide Garland

Beautiful Yuletide decorations may be made by weaving a garland from Blackthorn twigs, and decorating it with evergreens and bright berries abundant in the hedgerows at this time. On New Year's Day (some say on Twelfth Night) they should be taken down and burnt, and the ashes scattered in the fields to ensure a good crop at the following harvest.

Sloes vary in size from
15-30mm, are bluish-
purple, ripening to black,
with a powdery "bloom"

Flower buds form on spines during
winter. Next year flowers, then
leaves emerge as spines lengthen
and become small branches.

Some trees have small tightly
packed bunches of blossom -
some have a more open habit

Pure white flowers - five petals

Pale green anthers, yellowish
pollen tips, become orange
then brown as they mature

## NECTAR FROM THE BLACKTHORN TREE   by Brian Krengel

In April when I walk about through lanes and woods I steer
To see the spiny branches black before the leaves appear
And if they're covered in snowy flowers my heart is full of glee
For they will make the Nectar from the Blackthorn tree

In May I watch the weather and hope the gales don't blow
For heavy wind and rain the ground with little white flowers will strew
And then I know that there will be some hard old work for me
To gather sloes for Nectar from the Blackthorn tree

But if there's gentle showers and the breezes soft do blow
I'll turn unto my summer tasks and hope the sloes will grow
And while the Sun is ripening them and labour burdens me
I'll dream about the Nectar from the Blackthorn tree

Then in late September I make my way through nettles and bramble briars
With my stick and little bucket to gather the fruit so sour
And if in my bucket some handfuls of those purple jewels I see
I'll start to make the Nectar from the Blackthorn tree

Then in December when the Christmas season comes around
Through the streets some friends and I will make our carols sound
We'll need a little something our throats from coughs to ease
So we'll sip a little Nectar from the Blackthorn tree

Then the next year when the Spring Bank Holiday comes around
We'll hunt the Earl and bang our drums and make the Combe resound
On Monday night we'll shoot the Earl and throw him in the sea
And we'll share a little Nectar from the Blackthorn tree

# Hunting the Earl of Rone

The last verse of this song, that I added myself, refers to a custom celebrated in Combe Martin, North Devon for over 400 years, with a break between 1837 and 1974 having been banned as riotous! The story goes that in the 16th century the Earl of Tyrone, fleeing Ireland and pursued as a traitor, was washed up on the Devon coast and captured by the militia at Combe Martin. He was marched through the town, executed on the beach and his body thrown into the sea. A reasonable story perhaps, except it never happened! The Earl actually succeeded in sailing to Italy, and it is recorded that he lived in Rome to a ripe old age. It is interesting that a historical myth has been grafted on to similar West Country "coming of summer" ceremonies which feature an 'Oss (Hobby Horse), particularly those at Padstow, Cornwall and Minehead, Somerset on Mayday.

The Combe Martin revels, which now take place on the bank holiday weekend at the end of May, consist of a procession complete with Hobby Horse and "teaser" - a woman with a besom broom who dances around the 'Oss, attendant musicians and drummers (yes, that's me), and dozens of "flower maidens" dancing in rows back and forth across the road to lead the proceedings. We wind our way through the town "hunting" the Earl on Sunday, then on Monday evening the Earl is caught, and led, seated backwards on a donkey, down the main street. Every so often the procession stops, the Earl is shot by the Grenadiers, falls to the ground and is revived by the 'Oss and teaser, put back on the donkey and the procession resumes. While the Earl-shooting is going on, the musicians and drummers take a break and it has become customary to each carry a hip flask filled with our own home made tipple - mostly Sloe gin! We all sample each others offerings, and compare recipes in a great spirit of community. It all helps to keep us going- it's a long evening and the drums are heavy! - Oh my poor back!

# ELDER - RUIS

Letter - R
Number - 15
Rules - 25th November to 22nd December
13th lunar month

**Correspondences**

Element - Air & Water
Planet - Venus
Gender - Feminine
Bird - Rook
Beast - Badger
Deities - Dryads (tree spirits), Crone

**Interpretation**

Wisdom gained by experience that comes with age
not just facts and opinions - real knowledge

**Country names**

Poor Man's Medicine Chest
Queen of Herbs
Pipe Tree
Lady Ellhorn, Ellenwood

Elder

25th Nov
to
22nd Dec

Ruis

# Elder

25th Nov
to
22nd Dec

Shortly after moving to Sunnyside, we had to cut down a huge leylandii that was growing beside the back gate, far too close to the house. Almost immediately afterwards an Elder self-seeded (or was brought by a generous bird) and grew there, protecting our house. Every winter I prune this tree as it grows up to eight feet a year and would soon block the entrance and all the light out of the Kitchen as well! Before I cut, I always explain what I have to do and why, and I try to cut as cleanly and sympathetically as I can, and in return she has become a truly lovely tree. Each June there are blossoms as big as tea plates, sweet and musky, from which I make Elderflower cordial - the true taste of Summer! Then in September I'll make Elderberry rob for use as Cough mixture, or

# Ruis

diluted with hot water
as a warming winter
drink, and there
are always enough
berries left for
the birds too,
as well as
shelter from
the sparrowhawk!
It's like having
a benevolent
old grandmother
welcoming me
home whenever
I've been away.

# Elder - the Wisewoman

Now I have reached the end of the year, the 13th lunar month. The culmination of the mystical knowledge gained during the course of this time brings me to the Elder, which is associated with the Crone, the Wisewoman, and witches. As Wisewoman, she is the midwife who brings the New Year to birth. She is protective and healing, ancient and wise, with wisdom gained by experience, not just facts and opinions - real knowledge.

As protector, an Elder growing at the gate guards a home from evil and bad luck.

It is said that if this tree is cut down, it will bring disaster on the house. So always ask permission from the Lady before cutting elder -

*"Lady Ellhorn, give me some of thy wood, and I will give thee some of mine, when I become a tree"*

If Elder is burnt, calamity will strike-

*"Elder is the Lady's tree - burn it not or curst you'll be"*

But Elder is also a tree of the Faerie folk - old folklore states that children should not be laid in a cradle of Elder wood for fear of being taken by the faeries, or pinched black and blue by them. As Elder is a shrubby tree, and the branches are hollow, it does not grow much wood. It would have to be a very small cradle made from Elder wood, and a very small child to fit in it - possibly premature, so unlikely to survive.

# Legend of the Rollright Stones

**M**any years ago, in Oxfordshire, a King, ambitious to conquer England, was confronted by a witch at Little Rollright; she was Mother Shipton of Shipton - under - Wychwood, and seeing his greed, said to him;

*"Seven long strides thou shalt take,*
*and if Long Compton thou cans't see,*
*King of England thou shalt be"*

Long Compton, a village on the opposite side of the valley, was clearly visible from the top of the hill, so he confidently strode towards the summit, but at the last step a ridge of land, "The Arch Druid's Barrow", obscured Long Compton from his sight. The King was furious, but the witch declared;

*The King's Men, Rollright Stones*

*"As Long Compton thou cans't not see,*
*King of England thou shalt not be.*
*Rise up stick, stand still stone,*
*For King of England thou shalt be none.*
*Thou and thy men hoar stones shall be,*
*And I myself an Eldern tree"*

The King was transfixed where he stood and became the "King's stone", his men were transformed into the stone circle "the King's Men". The "Whispering Knights", another group of stones in a nearby field, were said by some to be treacherously plotting at the time, or by others, that they were at prayer. The witch remained as the Elder tree to guard the stones and protect the neighbouring countryside.

A picturesque story, similar to many romantic tales from 18th century.

# "Poor Man's Medicine Chest"

*Elder is famed for the many medicinal and healing properties of all its parts:*

*The berries and flowers can be used to induce sweating for a detoxifying effect.*

*Flowers will treat chilblains and stimulate the circulatory system.*

*Dried Leaves will act as an insecticide, also added to ointment for bruises and sprains.*

*To get rid of a wart, rub a green Elder twig on it then bury the twig in the ground. As the twig rots so the wart will disappear.*

*Elder branches grow extremely quickly, are virtually hollow, woody tubes filled with spongy pith that can be removed to form pipes – for magically blowing fire to life, or for musical whistles for use in ritual.*

143

Leaves emerge opposite in
pairs, 5 or 7 per stem. Buds
in axils. Flowers / berries in
groups of 3 or 4

Leaf stems emerge
opposite and alternately
North - South,
East - West

The pith which fills the hollow branches
has sleep inducing properties.

## Elderflower Cordial

The Taste of Summer - blooms
from May to the Summer Solstice.

10 - 12 heads Elderflowers
7 - 8 Litres Spring water
2 sliced Lemons
2 kilos Sugar
2 tablespoons Citric acid

As soon as the flowers are fully
open, on a warm sunny morning,
pick the Elderflowers and drop
them straight into the container
in which they are to be soaked in
enough cold spring water to easilly
cover them. Put a saucer on top to keep
the flowers under the water. Add the
sliced lemons, stir, and leave to soak
for 2 days. Strain through a sieve lined
with muslin. Add sugar and citric acid,
stir until all the sugar is dissolved. Pour into sterilised bottles and store in the fridge, it
will keep for up to 6 weeks. Dilute 1 part cordial to 3 parts water.

## Elderberry Rob

Pick complete heads of Elderberries when they are black and fully ripe, enough to quarter
fill a saucepan. Rinse, and then remove berries from the stalks with a fork. Boil gently for
10 mins in a large pan with 3 tablespoons water. Mash to release maximum juice. Pour
through a sieve, lined with muslin and discard flesh. For each pint of juice, add 1lb light
brown sugar. Boil 3 minutes. Pour into sterilised, warm bottles. As a cough syrup, take 1
or 2 teaspoons as needed. Or dilute with hot water for a soothing drink for sore throats.

# The Wisewoman of Felbridge

Having always been fascinated by herbal country remedies, I have grown herbs and gathered hedgerow ingredients for them for as long as I can remember. So I was amazed to discover that my great, great grandmother, born around 1860, had been a wisewoman and healer in Sussex around the late 19th and early 20th centuries. She made ointments, acted as a midwife and would also lay out the dead. Nanny - my grandmother (b.1902) had been sent out into the woods and lanes as a child, to collect the plants that her own grandmother used. But the old recipes were never written down, and no-one at the time wanted to learn, so when the old wisewoman died, the knowledge was lost.

I never knew about any of this until the day of Nanny's funeral in 1987, when I was in my early 30s. She was the last of her generation, and the final link with the Wisewoman of Felbridge. What I would have given for just a smattering of her knowledge.

It's curious isn't it? that many of the women in my family line, mother and daughter down the generations, to a greater or lesser degree, have had a talent for the practical healing arts, to each generation according to the spirit of the age.

My grandmother, living in semi rural wartime, was the one people called upon in times of need, knowing she would give practical help, and would not gossip about it afterwards. My mother, who lived in a suburban environment, was a member of St. John's Ambulance, a voluntary nurse in the local hospital and often helped neighbours in medical emergencies. I grew up in an age when what is now called "western medicine" was beginning to be questioned and "old ways" sought for the alternative wisdom that it's thought we'd lost. So it is not unexpected that I should be interested in herbs and run a wildlife rescue centre. And now, as alternative medicine has become so much more accessible, my own daughter practices several healing therapies too. I suppose healing is just like any other talent, be it musical or linguistic, athletic or scientific, it's in the genes and can be passed down along with blue eyes or curly hair!

# MISTLETOE
No Letter
No Number
Rules - 23rd December
the "day" of "a year and a day"

## Correspondences
Element - Fire
Planet - Sun
Metal - Gold
Gender - Masculine
Deities - the Sacrificial King, Balder

## Interpretation
Liminal space - Magic
Health, Fertility

## Country names
Golden Bough
Kissing Bough
Allheal

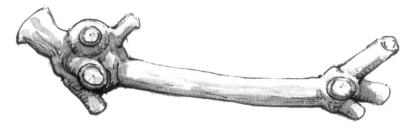

The Golden Bough

Misdetoe

23ʳᵈ Dec the "day" of "a year and a day"

Allheal

23rd December

These days at Yule/Christmas I hang the cards sent by friends and family around the living room walls and a bunch of Mistletoe, the biggest one I can find, in the middle of the room, in pride of place, where no-one can miss it. There it stays all year round, bringing harmony and love to the household, until 23rd Dec, the 'day' of 'a year and a day', when it is replaced by a new bunch. The old bunch is taken down and burnt ceremoniously in the hearth, and the ashes are sprinkled on the garden to help promote the magical properties of the herbs growing there. Some mistletoe grows in the trees around here, but the most spectacular is a huge bunch in a small

# MISTLETOE

# The 'day' of 'a year and a day' 23rd Dec

apple tree opposite the primary school in the village.
I always stop and look at it whenever I'm passing
that way - stunning!
For several years I've tried to
get Mistletoe to grow in the
old apple tree in our back
garden, I rub the sticky
berries into the bark, and
any crevices I can reach,
but no luck so far.
Maybe I should put
the berries on the lawn and
let the birds do the propagating
for me — they'd be better at it than
I am! Does the seed need to
pass through a bird's system
before it can germinate?

# 'The Golden Bough' 'Allheal'

# A Year and a Day

The Celtic lunar calendar reckoned the year in 13 months of 28 days = 364 days, so to complete the year an extra day was added - the "day" of "a year and a day". Ruled by Mistletoe, the most magical of all the trees in the Ogham, 23rd December is the extra day, as the year was said to end with the winter solstice, the 21st & 22nd December (counted twice, once each at the start and end of the year).

The Druids believed that Mistletoe was too sacred to be given a name or a symbol, but they called it "Allheal" because of its powerful medicinal properties.

A magical plant, not of the earth but growing between earth and sky, so that it forms a mystic link between them, Mistletoe is the 'Other', representing liminal space, that which is neither one thing nor another but which is the point of stillness between.

To the Celts, liminal space was the place where magic could happen, and all such places were sacred - dawn and dusk, the meeting of day and night; the sea shore where the land meets the sea; gateways and thresholds, all had mystical power. They were the separation between the physical and spiritual worlds, where access from one to the other was possible.

# The Golden Bough

Looking upwards into trees as they shed their leaves in storms of approaching winter, it is difficult not to be fascinated by sometimes huge bunches of mistletoe, growing on many an Apple tree, Poplar, Lime or Ash or sometimes the sacred Druids' tree, Oak. The Roman historian Pliny the Elder, wrote of Gaulish Druids in the year 77AD, describing a ceremony in which the priest, clad in a white robe, ascended the tree and cut the Mistletoe with a golden sickle, before passing it down to be caught in a white cloak. If the Mistletoe touched the ground, or was cut with iron, they believed that its magical properties would have been lost.

Mistletoe likes Apple best, displaying the male principal on a feminine host, representing balance and fertility. When found growing on an Oak tree, Mistletoe is doubly sacred, and potent masculine imagery, as the white berries are thought to be the semen of the Gods upon the regal Thunder King tree.

In his anthropological study of folklore and magic, 'The Golden Bough', James Frazer talks of Mistletoe growing on an oak as the phallus of the Sacrificial King, cut on 23rd December, the day of sacrifice when the king was ritually killed to return fertility to the land. The mistletoe bough was handed to the new chosen king as a symbol of his year of kingship, and so represents the power and responsibility of the royal state.

# The Kissing Bough

At Yuletide it is customary to make a Kissing Bough, which can vary from a single branch of Mistletoe to an elaborate decoration using two hoops, one thrust through the other, and bound around with evergreens, holly and ivy, and with apples specially reserved for the occasion. Inside are hung representations of male and female figures, and other brightly coloured baubles. At the bottom a bunch of mistletoe is carefully tied, and the whole tableau is suspended in the middle of the room, the centre of attention. Every berry on the mistletoe bears the promise of a kiss, an echo of the ancient fertility rite, and for every kiss given or taken a berry is removed. When all the berries are gone, the kissing has to stop!

*Mistletoe hung in the house all year round, till next year's branch is brought in, ensures protection from hunger and lightning (associations with thunder gods - Oak)*

*Berries - white, viscous, sticky, spread by birds (especially Mistle thrush)*

# Balder

The gentle Norse God Balder, son of Odin and Frigg, spread light and goodwill wherever he went, but was tormented by nightmares of death. So Frigg travelled throughout the nine worlds of the Universe and extracted oaths from everything, except the Mistletoe, that they would do no harm to her son. This put his fears to rest, but it soon became a sport among the Gods to throw spears and stones at him for the amusement of seeing them glance off the now "invulnerable" Balder. Eventually Loki, the trickster, discovered his one weakness, and gave the blind Hodr a sharp Mistletoe dart to throw, which killed Balder instantly. Distraught Frigg, trying to reverse the situation, dispatched her other son Hermod to Hel to offer a ransom for his brother. This would have been successful had not Loki refused to mourn for Balder, as everything else in the nine worlds did. It was later believed that, after Ragnarok, the doom of the Gods, Balder would return to rule over a beautiful green land, risen from the sea.

Another legend of the slain and risen king, which in this case reflects the transition of the year with the Mistletoe dart representing the catalyst for death and regeneration, as the extra day (Mistletoe's 23rd December) is the liminal space between one year and the next.

*A huge bunch of Mistletoe growing on the branch of a gnarled old apple tree down near the primary school in Sible. In late autumn when the leaves, what few there are left, are brown and dead the Mistletoe shines like a great golden beard.*

Lowers blood pressure and heart rate; eases anxiety, promotes sleep; relieves panic attacks and nervous headaches; improves concentration; prescribed for tinnitus and epilepsy; treats hyperactivity in children.

Mistletoe is now being tested as a possible cure for cancer, as Visco toxins in berries inhibit growth of some cancerous tumours and stimulate the immune system.

Caution – Mistletoe (especially berries) is highly toxic, and should only be used under medical supervision.

"They call the Mistletoe by a name meaning in their own language, the all healing" - Pliny.

New leaf stems grow in pairs between existing leaves. In some, a further pair develop on either side of new stems.

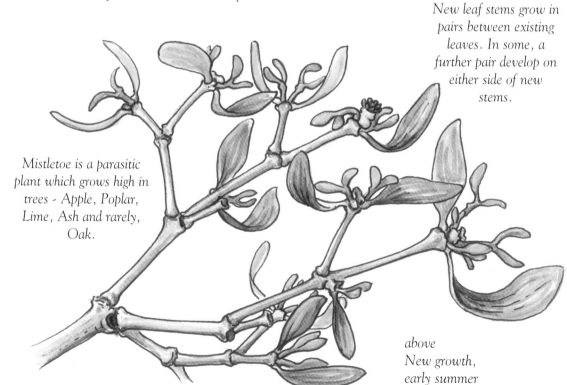

Mistletoe is a parasitic plant which grows high in trees - Apple, Poplar, Lime, Ash and rarely, Oak.

above
New growth,
early summer

# The Ogham Vowels

Having completed the year in lunar months, with each tree relating to one consonant in the alphabet, I have arrived at the section of the Ogham where trees relate to the vowels, of which there are five, also to the Solstices and Equinoxes, of which there are four. However, the Winter Solstice is both the start and the finish of the year, and the significance of these two is quite different, so it is counted twice, making five symbols.

Previously the significances of the trees have been fairly specific as archetypes. This time they are more fundamental, and relate not only to the year as a period of 365/6 days, one complete circuit of the earth around the sun; but also to the year as a representation of a human lifespan. This is separated into five stages: initially looking forward approaching life as a journey; secondly, recognising pitfalls which may be encountered; thirdly, encountering the Divine; fourthly, establishing a communication with the Divine particularly approaching the end of life; and lastly, preparing for and making the transition from this life to the next.

# SCOTS PINE - AILM

Letter - A
Number - 16
Rules - Winter Solstice at the start of the year
22nd December

**Correspondences**
Element - Earth & Air
Planet - Mars
Gender - Masculine
Cardinal point - East
Bird - Lapwing
Beast - Deer
Deities - Attis, Cybele, Dionysus

**Interpretation**
A signpost at the start of the year, pointing the way
Guidance

Scots Pine

22nd Dec
Winter
Solstice
start of year

Ailm

# Scots Pine

A bitterly cold afternoon, snow threatening, grey and damp, Northeast wind, waxing moon. I knew there were Scots Pines at Gosfield church and fully intended to go there, but as I drove, for some reason I got sidetracked and turned into the car park at Broaks Wood, a mixed wood, about a mile in each direction, and half a mile from home on the other side of the main road. It is virgin ancient woodland, partly cropped for timber, and was mentioned in a charter in 1191. It's criss-crossed with way marked trails for the use of walkers, and gets lots of visitors. I was looking at a tree, trying to decide if it was a Scots Pine or some other variety, when I met a neighbour whose house backs onto the woods. She told me an amazing story about coming face to face with a Red deer Stag outside her back door a few nights before, and wasn't really sure which of them had been more Shocked! I walked up the main path into the wood, and before long came across Simon Leatherdale, the forester, burning waste at the hut. I stopped and talked for a while, exchanging family news — our daughters

# Winter Solstice
## Start of the Year
### 22nd Dec

# Ailm

had been friends at school, and we talked about the local deer, the little solitary Muntjak, Roe, Fallow, and a herd of Red deer that roam for miles. When I told him what I was there for he said there was some Scots Pine down by the car park, and offered to cut a branch for me, so I jumped into his pickup and he drove me back down the track. It was the tree I'd been looking at when I met Val. It had a few branches with cones on, but way out of reach, at least twenty feet up.

Luckily, foresters carry all sorts of gear, including long loppers. Just as well I hadn't gone to Gosfield!

# The Journey

Here I must make a mental adjustment to return to the Winter Solstice at the very beginning of the year, to the Scots Pine, a signpost pointing the way, a guide at the start of the year's journey.

The tall Pine stands above the distractions of life, which crowd around at the foot of the tree among the leaf litter. He sees far into the distance, and marks the way, aloof and guiding, protecting and reviving but above all far-seeing. Scots Pines were often planted in small groups of 2 or 3 on 'sighting points', either ley lines or on tumuli, and may have been used to navigate great distances across the ancient landscape, following from one signpost to the next at a point on the horizon.

Scots Pine is the signpost pointing the way to the future, to what must be done to truly achieve potential, to make sense of life. Life is the journey, and the trick is to think of the journey as every bit as important as the destination, but keeping the distant goal in sight so there is something to aim for. Any journey consists of hundreds of single steps, but taking each of those steps consciously and knowing the detail of the path taken, is to learn something new and exciting with every step! If you can take notice of the primroses on the path, and see how the sunlight falls on the petals, the particular shade of greeny-grey of the shadows beneath them, smile to yourself at the joy that sight brings and then move on, holding onto the joy, but striding onwards, then you've cracked it!

I always take pleasure in the tiny things, but if I find that I am walking aimlessly in circles, getting nowhere, I look for the distant goal, the Pine tree. All the way-markers are there to be seen, it's just a question of remembering to look for them and keeping to the overall purpose of reaching the next signpost on the horizon. Eventually you will look back and be amazed at how far you have come.

**Scots Pine** *is the only true native pine, thought to be the first tree to establish after the ice age.*

*A very tall young tree is conical but as it ages the lower branches die off leaving a bare trunk and higher growth becomes flattened to leave a distinctive outline*

*Needles in pairs about three inches long.*

*Cones take three years to mature.*

*In damp conditions cones remain tightly closed, but open in dry weather to expose winged seeds between the scales, releasing them on to the wind.*

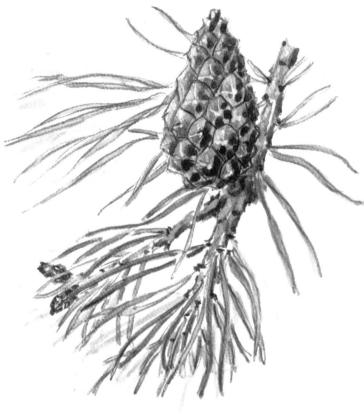

*Pine resin - used in wax polish, pitch, antiseptic.*
*When used to seal boats, the protection of Poseidon is invoked.*

# Revived Fertility

As the Winter Solstice stands at the lowest point of the cycle of the Sun, it is also the start of the renewal of the Sun's power, so Scots Pine is associated with the slain and risen God. In many ancient traditions, the evergreen Pine tree kept alive the spirit of vegetation throughout the winter, reviving it the following spring. This custom of decorating a Pine tree in the winter was revived in Victorian England with the popularisation of the Christmas tree from Germany by Prince Albert.

Part of the cult of the ancient Great Earth Mother Goddess Cybele (which spanned a period from 1500 b.c.e until Roman times and an area from Anatolia - modern Turkey- through Greece and Crete to Rome itself) involved her son-lover Attis who at death transformed himself into a Pine tree with violets springing from the earth where his blood fell. At the Phrygian festival of Cybele (in Anatolia), the Pine tree was decorated with violets and carried into the Phrygian Sanctuary, where it remained for three days. After this time the Pine Tree disappeared, and Attis was said to have returned to life. Is this a forerunner of the Christian Easter?

The phallic pine cone on top of Dionysus' pine wand, the "tree-egg", was the symbol of renewed fertility and has echoes in the Green Man, returning life to the earth.

The cycles of life, death and rebirth are central to the Wheel of the Year, and can be seen in the Ogham as a theme that has returned over and over again, encouraging everyone to strive to become one with the cycles of life, and the ebb and flow of the seasons. To help achieve this, try boiling pine needles in almond oil for use in massage (calming and cleansing), or put aside a special time for contemplation, and use it as a bath oil.

# GORSE - ONN

Letter - O
Number - 17
Rules - Spring Equinox
21st March

**Correspondences**
Element - Fire
Planet - Sun
Gender - Masculine
Bird - Cormorant
Beast - Hare
Deities - Sun Lord
Cailleach

**Interpretation**
Passion, Promiscuity, Corruption

**Country names**
Furze
Whinn
"Gorst" - Anglo Saxon meaning wasteland

gorse

21$^{st}$ Mar
Spring
Equinox

Onn

# Gorse

Awoke to a sprinkling of snow on the ground, which melted as soon as the sun shone though it was still cold till lunchtime. Mid afternoon. I walked east, half a mile up the lane from home, across the small stream and came out on the main road. On the opposite side is The Brooks, where I went in search of Gorse. First I spent some time walking round the wood, doing a few sketches and just enjoying the peace, but I was a bit horrified at the state of the place this time. There was rubbish strewed along the main path, and deep in the woods, the remains of a bonfire surrounded by litter - so sad, a desecration -

**ONN** the result of unguarded passion. When I came back to the car park, the sun was warm and low. I sat on a log to draw the gorse bushes. The contrast from the mornings snow was marked. It felt as if the point of balance between the cold and warm halves of the year had tipped on this Spring Equinox day, when day and night are of equal length. There are loads of flowers on the gorse and masses of buds. The spines were stiff and sharp, it was difficult and somewhat painful to cut. I felt a sullen resentment - when I had asked, there had been no response, Now I felt I was not welcome. There is a bit of the gypsy about gorse, often growing in wild places; it's prickly, jealous of its independence, its otherness, gaudy in its colours, its bright sunny yellow flowers contrast with its dark bitter green spines. It keeps intruders away, but protects its own, and woe betide any who don't approach with care and a measure of respect!

# Passions and Pitfalls

Gorse is the shrubby tree which represents the Spring Equinox, the second vowel, and in the section of the Ogham that teaches life lessons, it shows the pitfalls which may be encountered on the journey.

Gorse flowers mainly in the spring and summer, but all year round there are some blooms to be seen, and its prickly spines are always sharp. The saying "When gorse is in bloom, kissing is in season" may be interpreted as a licence to self-indulgence, but in fact this is a warning to beware the heady scent of springtime (youth), because that is where great dangers may lie. Appetites and desires are drawn from instincts designed to encourage vital activities (eating, drinking, sex etc.), and are naturally innocent. However, when any appetite is excessively indulged it can result in unpleasant consequences (e.g. eating disorders, alcoholism, unwanted pregnancy and disease). Self control needs to be cultivated or instilled at a reasonably early age, as it is likely to engender self respect. The alternative is that balance in life can be lost. Passions and emotions allowed to run out of control can become obsessions, anger can give rise to violence, infatuation may lead to stalking or rape, unguarded spending can cause unmanageable debt and any of these may result in ruin and ultimately even imprisonment.

The lesson is to not be seduced by hedonism. If strong passions or emotions are allowed to take over then Gorse will prick and hurt you, and you will have to refocus or you'll end up trapped in a vicious cycle of compulsive behaviour, from which help may be needed to escape. The answer is "moderation in all things", have fun, enjoy yourself, but don't overdo it! If self control is not learnt during childhood or the early days of independent adulthood it may take a long time to unravel the consequences. It is inevitable that we all make mistakes, but by thinking of the consequences of your actions, hopefully they won't be big ones!

# Wild places

*Gorse from 'Gorst', Anglo Saxon = waste land*
*Heath = wild place often overgrown with gorse*
*Heathen = heath dweller - dweller in wild places - country dweller*
*Pays = countryside (French), Pagan = country dweller*

Gorse is associated with wild places where meetings for sabbats, the rituals of the Old Religion at the Equinoxes and Solstices, could take place without attracting prying outsiders. Beltane 'bringing in the May', or the Autumn Equinox 'Nutting', were opportunities for young people to celebrate the changing seasons in the way young people always had, staying out all night for secret assignations and frolics!

In spring, Gorse provides safe nesting places, protecting the young birds and their mothers from predators, and also provides food for bees, before most other flowers are in bloom.

# Spring Equinox

Gorse rules the Spring Equinox, a time when "Mad March Hares" box in the fields by the light of the Full Moon. Some say this is to compete with rivals for a mate, while others think it is part of the courtship ritual to strengthen the pair bond. The Hare is thought to have been the original "Easter Bunny", but rabbits live in burrows, while hares shelter in shallow scrapes in the ground in open fields. This may have given rise to the old belief that hares lay eggs, mistaking ground nesting bird's eggs for the produce of the hares who share the same land; it's easy to see where the Easter egg originates! It is also interesting to note that the date of the Christian Easter is still reckoned as the first Sunday after the first Full Moon after the Spring Equinox, how pagan is that?

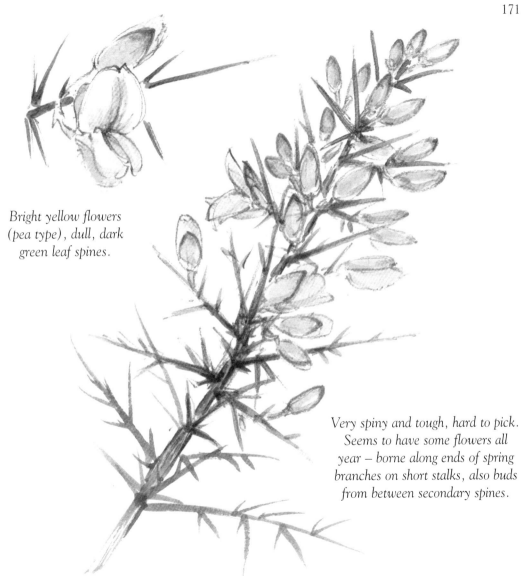

Bright yellow flowers
(pea type), dull, dark
green leaf spines.

Very spiny and tough, hard to pick.
Seems to have some flowers all
year – borne along ends of spring
branches on short stalks, also buds
from between secondary spines.

# Cormorants and Calendars

The totem bird of Gorse is the Cormorant, also known as the Sea Crow, and associated with the Crone aspect of the Goddess. "Cailleach" is her Celtic name. Cailleach day is the 25th March (around the Spring Equinox), also known as Lady Day, and was once celebrated widely as New Year's Day. For some people this is a reflection of summer's victory over darkness, but the reality is more practical / historical.

Julius Caesar's (Julian) calendar (45 b.c.e.) was introduced to standardise the reckoning of the years across the Roman Empire. The New Year, which had been 1st March, was redesignated as 1st January. Later, when Christianity spread, biblical events were assigned dates by the Church. Christmas day was settled on the 25th December, and was for a time also called New Year, but counting back nine months (25th March - Lady Day) to the Annunciation, others argued that the conception of Jesus should be the start of the Christian year. And so it remained for several centuries with Julian and Christian calendars operating side by side, until the Gregorian calendar was introduced by Pope Gregory in 1582, again attempting to standardise across the western world and removing 11 days to re-align with the solar year.

Again 1st January was designated as New Year's Day. However, many Protestant countries totally ignored this new Popish calendar and so confusion continued. But though 25th March was considered the start of the year, the 1st January had still been called New Years Day by many across Europe for centuries! Eventually in 1752 the calendar was reformed in Britain, and the Gregorian system was officially recognised, with attendant rioting by people who thought the new calendar had shortened their lives by 11 days (see also Page 57). The confusion wasn't quite over yet. Much of the civil administration, originally done by clerical monks, still held to the pre reformation system, and kept 25th March as its new year, but with the new calendar and the 11 day difference, that then became by modern reckoning 6th April, where it has remained to this day as the start of the tax year!

*Early summer. Seed pods forming. New growth springs from below flowering stems*

"When Gorse is in bloom, kissing is in Season"
- Gorse blooms all year round!

*Old seed pod*

*Flowers make good wine, also used to flavour whisky. Gorse flower tea is diuretic.*

# HEATHER - UR

Letter - U
Number - 18
Rules - Summer Solstice
21st June

**Correspondences**
Element - Water
Planet - Venus
Gender - Feminine
Bird - Lark
Beast - Bee
Deities - Cybele, Isis & Osiris, Venus
Uroica - Gallic Goddess (Erica - Latin name of Heather)

**Interpretation**
Solitude and communion with the Divine
Change, cleansing, new patterns of behaviour
Transformation
Uncertainty, overthrowing, dispersal

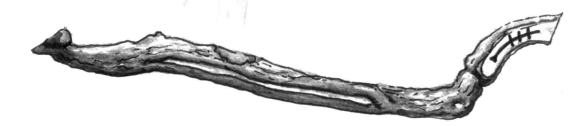

heather

21ˢᵗ Jun
Summer
Solstice

UR

# heather

Mid evening, still, calm, clear, sun setting.
OK. so every rule has an exception, and
this is it. I really tried to make the whole
Ogham learning thing a close to home experience,
but there just isn't any Heather near home so—
I'm sitting on the edge of a sheepfold on the high
Heather moors above Lofthouse in North Yorkshire
— I happened to be up here working at a trade fair.
It is a circular drystone shelter, sunk into the
ground, with a 6ft diameter floor of stone flags
2 or 3ft below ground level and about 2ft of wall
above, covered with lichen and with heather growing
between the stones. The entrance is a narrow gap
on the south east side. There is no roof, but it
must provide good shelter for a dozen or so sheep
in bad weather. Though there appears to be no
drainage, it would certainly keep sheep alive in
deep snow, crowded together their shared body heat
would be almost cozy. A place apart.

# Summer Solstice 21st June

# UR

At first it seemed to be quiet, but once I'd settled down and begun to listen, the whole place was full of noises. Suddenly I'm hearing curlews, grouse, pheasant and some sort of "seep-seep" lark-looking bird. The warm sun is sinking. Distant unseen sheep, sounding almost like ghosts of all the sheep that have ever been here, are bleating across the moor. Curlews are calling constantly. I've just been 'buzzed' by two snipe whooshing past my right ear, then charging on towards the sunset. It's not quiet at all, but it is really peaceful; solitude. I feel I could sit here forever, surrounded by heather and birds, just soaking in the peace and communing with the spirits of this place.

# Solitude and Fire

*Heather (Heath) means solitude*
*Heather grows in wild places,*
*Heathen = heath dweller = dweller in wild places*

Growing mainly in wilder less accessible places Heather is the Ogham symbol most associated with solitude. Heathery places are often wild with few people, a place for reflection and contemplation, a place where it is possible to encounter the Divine, whatever the Divine is perceived to be.

*Deep peace of the running wave to you*
*Deep peace of the flowing air to you*
*Deep peace of the shining stars to you*
*Deep peace of the quiet earth to you*
*Deep peace of the son of peace to you*
*A Celtic Benediction*

Peace may be found in solitude and in wild places in a way that is hard to capture in the hustle and bustle of daily life, but once that peace has been experienced, it can be held safe inside to be called on, whenever it's needed. It is the peace that enables centring on the spirit inside each of us and to make the connection to the Great Spirit that some call God and others call the mass consciousness or family soul of the human race. Once the connection is made any number of psychic activities may be unlocked - prayer, meditation, healing, clairvoyance, magic…

To make the connection is to "centre", to draw consciousness inwards, away from the external physical world, shrinking your attention until it focuses on a point within your own self. To me it is a point inside my head which is like a small door that opens to enable me to draw in a stream of something- life force, spirit, I don't know what to call it, but as it washes through my body it feels like cool refreshing water, and as it reaches my extremities, it makes my hands and sometimes my lips tingle, becoming a physical manifestation of a spiritual force. Then this force can be focused to achieve a healing process either in myself or passed into another person or creature, and can even be sent for use in distant healing. Physical limitations do not seem to apply; visualisation and intention seem to have the same effect on spirit as physical impetus has on objects.

In order to achieve the state of mind to make the initial contact many people employ ritual, calling on Deities, saints, ancestors, elements etc. to be present and help in the work. Coloured robes and candles, incense, music and chanting, or language and speech tone and pattern all aid the directing of visualisation necessary to make the shift to spiritual consciousness. Elaborate lists of correspondences will provide material for designing rituals for specific purposes, and I also use these for imagery in my artwork. Many religions have adopted this approach but often the result in the congregation is more likely to be a mere psychological bonding, establishing community rather than communion. This may be because individuals have never been taught how to make the transition, and act only as onlookers in a large group pageant. I have been a solitary practitioner for most of my adult life, having decided that ritual did not quite do it for me, but it would be interesting to see how much power is raised in a small group, who have worked closely together for years, and can "centre" communally.

Heather regenerates after fire, clearing old growth and encouraging germination by the cleansing heat. Fire is in itself a potent force for transformation; it turns clay into pots and raw meat into food, it makes things more useful. In the imagery of the spirit, fire is the force that cleanses and transforms the personality from the standard base state into the higher spiritually active state. But as fire can burn, the transformation is sometimes difficult and may be painful, it takes hard and consistent work to achieve, and unsympathetic influences in life may have to be removed.

When one spends time in solitude, meditating on matters of the spirit, the cleansing effect of spiritual fire can be felt, clearing away much of the accumulated ephemera of ordinary life and allowing spiritual development to take place. It is the essence of Retreat.

In divination, Heather means cycles of change, new patterns and transformation, uncertainty and insecurity, and the overthrowing of old established ways, dispersal. This is the natural consequence of the successful retreat, as new patterns of being emerge with the growing awareness of the spiritual nature of life, and going forward, maybe with some trepidation into the unknown.

*Gnarled and dead, bleached by sun
and water, this trunk has almost
the quality of stone or bone.*

New growth is bright green with pinkish tips

Shoots bear leaf scales on four sides, giving a concave diamond shaped cross section

Each heather plant looks like a tree in miniature, with a gnarled and twisted trunk, some only a few inches long, some up to 18", giving way to branches spreading in a tangled knot, then twigs bearing tiny scale-like leaves and flowers.

# Nectar from the Gods

Heather's totem creature is the bee, who loves nectar and makes much honey from the high moorland Heather. Bees are said to orientate themselves between hive and Heather navigating by way of the Sun, and were regarded by the Celts as messengers travelling the path of the Sun to the spirit world returning with messages from the Gods. In ancient times the priests of Cybele, the Great Earth Mother of Phrygia, in a state of ecstasy, castrated themselves to become the drones of their Goddess as Queen Bee.

I always look forward to seeing the Heather as I approach the North York Moors every August on the way to Whitby Folk Week. All over the moors there are standing stones and waymarkers bearing messages for the traveller, like the messages carried by bees from the Gods. By midsummer the whole moor is purple and glows with the heather blossom - imagine the number of bees it must take to pollinate all that? The sheer scale of the labour is awe-inspiring. The attribute most associated with bees is hard, unceasing work, and the reward for this work is the sweet honeycomb that supports and feeds the colony. Honey is healing and soothing, and beeswax is used in making ointments, so whenever I eat honey, I silently thank the bees that made it, and think gratefully of their industrious labours.

*High Bridestones on the North York Moors.*

Heathery Moors are wild, a place
for reflection and contemplation,
a place where it is possible to
encounter the Divine

# WHITE POPLAR - EADHA

Letter - E
Number - 19
Rules - Autumn Equinox
21st September

**Correspondences**

Element - Air & Fire
Planet - Sun
Gender - Masculine
Bird - Swan
Deities - Heracles
Underworld Gods

**Interpretation**

Oracle
Emotional connection with the Divine
Safe passage to and from the Otherworld

White Poplar

21ˢᵗ Sept
Autumn
Equinox

Eadha

# White ⸸ Poplar

Autumn Equinox - Warm, sunny, west wind.
I walked down the lane, past the black barn, to the
airfield. It was a lovely afternoon. As I passed 'my'
Rowan, she seemed most dishevelled, with deer-nibbled
bark, broken twigs, generally rather scruffy. I'd got my
secateurs in my pocket, so I did a bit of pruning and
untangled a couple of branches that were rubbing
against each other. When I had finished, she looked a
better shape, with the chance of healthier and tidier
growth — she seemed a bit
happier!

At the end of the old concrete runway there's a big muckheap where I've watched deer play "King of the castle". I carried on, past the muckheap and up to the hedge where the white Poplars grow. I was concentrating on which tree to approach, then which branch to ask for to make my Ogham stick. I was shown a branch of the right thickness just above my head, typically grey and knobbly, and cut it carefully, thinking "what can I do for you in return?" At the base of the trunk, caught among the undergrowth at the hedge bottom, were a couple of supermarket carrier bags. As the wind shakes Poplar's leaves, they are said to whisper with the voice of the divine, but with the plastic rattling and rustling so loudly, Eadha couldn't possibly hear the voices! So it was obvious what I had to do. I carried away the noisy rubbish, and as I said thankyou and goodbye, the west mind replied with a soft "sssshhh.." in the branches above me.

**21st Sept Autumn Equinox eadha**

# Whispers and Memories

White Poplar, the Ogham symbol for the Autumn Equinox ushers in the shorter days and darker nights. The year is approaching its dusk, but with a warm evening still to look forward to. If Heather has led to an encounter with the Divine, it is through the guidance of the Poplar that this communication is developed - both through listening and discourse. Poplars - White, Black, and Aspen are all closely related, and in mythology tend to occur as alternatives but with similar interpretations and imagery. The broad leaves of Poplar are born on long, flexible stalks which cause them to flutter with the slightest movement of the air. They are in constant movement and seem to shimmer in the breeze, causing the leaves to whisper. Poplars teach us to listen to the voice of the Divine, which surrounds us at all times and in all places, only stillness and attention is required in order to hear. The emotional quality to this spiritual connection is signified by the quaking and shaking of the leaves.

If we can, we should journey fearlessly into the otherworld to discover the secrets of existence and return as Heracles did with a great spiritual prize. In Greek mythology, beside the Pool of Memory, the waters of which may give recollection of previous incarnations to those who drink, grows the Aspen tree from whose leaves Heracles wove a crown to allow him to cross the river Styx and travel to the underworld safely. There he captured the three headed hound Cerberus, and returned again to the waking world. It is said that those who cross over the River Styx lose all memory of the land of the living, but because Heracles had discovered the secret of the Aspen tree he was able to defy the ancient law. Crowns of golden aspen leaves have been found in burial mounds in Mesopotamia dated to around 300 b.c.e. They were thought to have been worn by heroes, but also to allow the dead to be safely reborn. The heat of Heracles' brow scorched the underside of the leaves of his crown white, which is why it is said to this day

leaves downy
pale green on top
silvery white below

May
seed pods
split to reveal white downy seeds

developing floret buds →

white poplar
April
flowers = long tassles of small
bright yellow florets

the leaves of Poplar trees are darker above and white below. Heracles' last labour may be seen as a shamanic journey, travelling into the otherworld, and returning with a magical prize, having gained immortality.

*The leaves of Poplar trees are darker above and white below, this can be seen as an expression of the duality of all things: life / death; light / darkness; day / night; male / female; right / left; physical / spiritual.*

# Making a Spiritual Journey

Making a shamanic journey, exploring the world of spirit, is a form of meditation. I find it best to take some time alone, at least 20 minutes when I'm undisturbed, and can settle myself comfortably either sitting in an upright chair with armrests, or laying on my back on a bed. For some people hypnotic or calming music may help to shut out external distractions. I start by closing my eyes and breathing slowly and deeply, concentrating on the breathing for a few minutes to quieten my mind's activity. Once this is achieved I can direct my attention to the journey. In my imagination, I pass through an intermediate place, crossing a river, or descending a staircase - any other scenario that seems right - this is the liminal space between the physical world and the world of spirit, the threshold of the otherworld. Having passed into the otherworld I just watch and see what happens. To be completely honest I usually fall asleep! I've been trying for years, but I'm really not very good at it, but once in a while something quite spectacular happens. Halfway through the year in which I was first studying the Ogham I fell asleep in the middle of a meditation and had a dream which seemed important, though I had no idea why immediately. As soon as I awoke I wrote it down in my diary. This is what I wrote:

*Some sort of College / Museum - on my way to fetch someone, I descended a wooden staircase into a gallery full of display cases. At the bottom of the stairs, tucked into a corner, was a pile of objects, boxes, books etc. On top was a sheet of old crumpled paper with written on it "with a Birch and a Beech and a Big Stick". Under the paper was a wooden shield with two pieces of wood (Birch and Beech) in the shape of horns, smoothed with constant rubbing, mounted above a mouth - toothy, horse like, a rough hewn stick clasped between the teeth.*

*Birch = beginnings, journey, quest.*
*Beech = learning, knowledge, same root as "book", foundation.*
*Big Stick = force, threatening, determination.*

This dream happened at a time when the research I was doing with the trees was becoming difficult due to the demands of work. I had almost stalled, and the dream gave me the determination to continue. At the time I interpreted it as "Don't you dare stop now, you've started the learning, keep going!"

*White Poplar leaves, shiny green above, velvety white below. Long flexible, flattened stems*

Several years on I have become aware of many layers of meaning which have gradually dawned on me, and the more I think about it, the more I find.

If all this sounds a bit "off the wall", that is because, in our modern world, we are encouraged to disregard anything that cannot be proved, measured or labelled. However, great mystics and spiritual leaders have always talked about such things - for them the otherworld is real. As children, we all lived in an "imaginary" world some of the time; it is a shame that as adults this creative ability is systematically stifled until most people believe it is simply fantasy.

Perhaps as old age approaches and demands of family and career start to recede, there is time to explore again the boundaries of reality, and to decide for yourself what you really believe in.

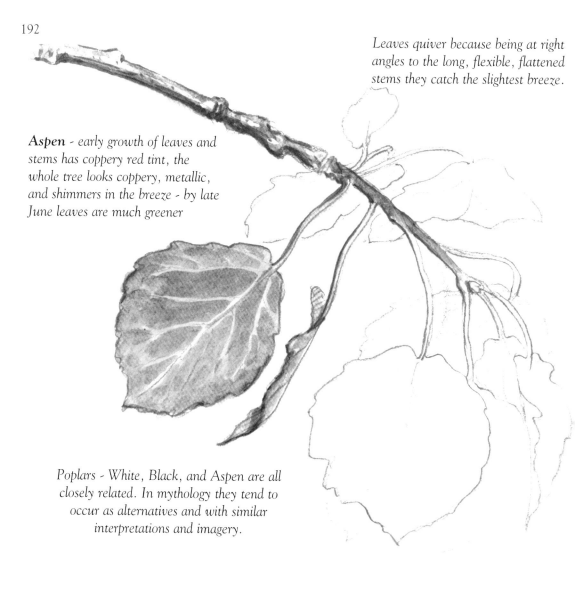

Leaves quiver because being at right angles to the long, flexible, flattened stems they catch the slightest breeze.

**Aspen** - early growth of leaves and stems has coppery red tint, the whole tree looks coppery, metallic, and shimmers in the breeze - by late June leaves are much greener

Poplars - White, Black, and Aspen are all closely related. In mythology they tend to occur as alternatives and with similar interpretations and imagery.

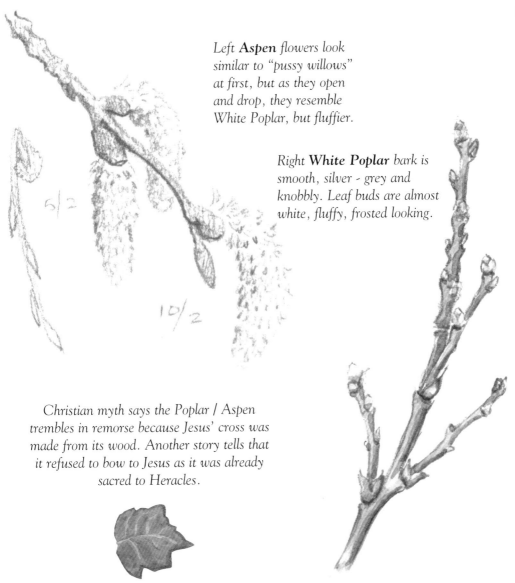

*Left **Aspen** flowers look similar to "pussy willows" at first, but as they open and drop, they resemble White Poplar, but fluffier.*

*Right **White Poplar** bark is smooth, silver - grey and knobbly. Leaf buds are almost white, fluffy, frosted looking.*

*Christian myth says the Poplar / Aspen trembles in remorse because Jesus' cross was made from its wood. Another story tells that it refused to bow to Jesus as it was already sacred to Heracles.*

# YEW - IOHO
Letter - I
Number - 20
Rules - Winter Solstice at the end of the year
21st December

## Correspondences
Element - Earth & Water
Planet - Saturn
Gender - Feminine
Bird - Eagle
Deities - Hecate, Hades & Persephone
The Fates

## Interpretation
The Wheel of life, death and rebirth
Transformation
A guide at the threshold

Yew

21st Dec
Winter
Solstice
end of year

Ioho

# yew

18th Dec. Midday, freezing cold, clear, icy.
When my daughter Aly was at primary school
she was taken on a class trip to The Broaks,
and the children were taught about the wildlife
in the woods, shown the bat nesting boxes and
Badger sets, and each 'adopted' a tree.
Today I walked to the woods to collect pine cones for
Yule decorations, with Colin and Aly, who showed us
the secret places, and introduced us to 'her' tree -
a Scots Pine, deep in the woods. We'd walked up the
main path and round the north edge of the wood,
when we came across a lone Yew tree, with a log
pulled up against the trunk. I sat down. After a
few moments I started to feel dizzy and
disorientated, this must be the effect I had
heard about of the fumes from the hallucinogenic
sap.

It would have been interesting
to see what would
have happened if
I'd stayed longer!
No time now –
I must come back
at the Solstice
and try
again.

I did go back
– for my 2nd
visit to Ioho
see the Epilogue
at the end of
the book.

21st Dec  end of the Year  Ioho
Winter Solstice

# Poison and Protection

*Taxus = Yew (Latin)*
*Toxon = bow (Greek)*
*Toxicon = Poison (Greek), poison for arrows*
*Toxic = poisonous*

All parts of the Yew are poisonous to a greater or lesser degree. Live foliage may be grazed in small quantities by most animals, but after being cut, toxic chemicals start to build up in the dead leaves, and may prove fatal if eaten. Yew berries have a red fleshy coating, which is mostly harmless if ingested in small amounts, but it surrounds a highly poisonous seed. This passes intact through most birds to no ill effect, but will however cause severe bleeding and inflammation of the digestive tract of all animals, and eventually kill them if the kernel is absorbed. Yew bark, poisonous if eaten, is said to give off hallucinogenic fumes, and death may result if exposure is prolonged.

The wood of the Yew tree is close grained and elastic (and very hard to cut!), the best wood for longbows, so during medieval times, they were planted by decree in churchyards, as this was considered the centre of the village community, but also to avoid harm to domestic animals by preventing them from browsing on the poisonous foliage.

Because of its association with death and transition, many Yew trees are thought to have marked ancient sites of pre Christian worship.

When Christianity came, Yews were incorporated into the grounds of early Christian churches, many of them built on existing sacred sites. Whatever the origins of Yew trees growing in churchyards, many old tales tell of the protective role of the tree in relation to those buried there. It is said that a root of the Yew tree grows into the mouth of every corpse buried in the graveyard and protects and preserves the spirit until rebirth or the day of judgement.

# Life, Death and Rebirth

Yew is the Ogham symbol for the Winter Solstice at the end of the year. When I made my second visit to the Yew tree in the Broaks I was conscious both of this and of coming to the conclusion of a phase in my Ogham project. Research was nearly over; designs were following closely and I had kept a diary. Would this be the end of things or would the project come to life again later in a different form? At this point I didn't know. Yew was both a conclusion and possibly a point of transition into something new.

Perhaps most appropriately, Yew is the longest lived of all native trees. After many centuries, its central trunk becomes hollow, and a new tree may be born and grow within the dead trunk. Sometimes the drooping branches, where they touch the ground may root and send up new growth to eventually become a ring of young trees - the next generation, but in fact an extension of the original tree. Yew illustrates perfectly the continuing cycles of life, death and rebirth, which brings me neatly to the final lesson the Ogham has to teach. Life and death are two sides of the same coin. If death is the final phase of this physical life, it is also the threshold to whatever is to follow, an event that I would like to think can be approached with wonder, curiosity and anticipation; and can be experienced as fully as almost anything else in life.

At this stage in my life (in my 50s)I don't quite feel qualified to talk in any great detail about approaching death, as I have only very limited experience of it. But I don't understand why society as a whole seems so frightened by it, and I can only say what I would like my own death to be like.

It is a shame that in the modern western world, death is very much a taboo subject and people are often propelled to their end unprepared, frightened, drugged and alone, as if modern urban societies find death rather embarrassing and a bit of a nuisance - How can that be good? It is rather a mark of the extent to which modern living has become dislocated from the natural rhythms of life. It has created fear of the unknown, which is the worst thing anyone can face.

As with a woman approaching childbirth 'naturally', I think that if death can be accepted as a 'natural' event and prepared for, who knows what kind of rewarding spiritual experience it could be! Wouldn't it be good to reach the transition in a peaceful environment, with the presence of sympathetic attendants, friends and family, after a full and rewarding life? One would be able to give oneself over to consciously trusting in the strength of ones own spirit to make the transition naturally. I hope it will be like that for me.

In the "Tibetan Book of the Dead" is a Buddhist ceremony in which the words of the *Bardo Thodol* are spoken into the ear of the dying person, giving a reassuring and comprehensive guide to the various stages of transition the spirit will encounter between life and death, which, if made well, will ensure a peaceful passage to the next life and a fortunate reincarnation. Guidance is also given to the attendants. For those within this spiritual tradition, this must be a beautiful option both for those dying and their companions.

Then when we get to the other side, and become part of the spirit world ourselves, everything will become clear, BUT - will we suddenly realise that we have completely missed the point?

Early summer - tufts of new leaves will extend and grow into new branches

Leaves grow from alternating bracts in four positions around the stem in a spiral formation. 4 is the number of completion - 4 seasons, 4 cardinal points, Spiral = life (DNA)

December - flesh of fruits diminishes and shrinks away to reveal seeds

The name "Yew" may be derived from a Greek word meaning "to arrange", as the leaves are neatly arranged on either side of the twigs.

The Wheel of Life, Death and Rebirth has now come full circle. The Yew is the longest living tree, which can regenerate itself to survive for thousands of years, and so represents life, but the Yew tree's province is also death (poison), and rebirth (after spirits in the graveyard are preserved).

So the year of the Ogham is complete, and again I find myself returning from a visit to Ioho, through the Broaks, and past the car park, but here's Ailm, the Scots Pine, pointing the way to another cycle, another year, another life . . .

# Epilogue

New Year's Day, 1st January, noon, sunny, fine, very muddy in the wood - it had been raining on and off for several days.

Finally managed to find time to make my visit to the Yew tree in the Broaks with Colin. During the walk we talked about the visit and I asked him to help with the practicalities - keep watch, return after twenty minutes and rouse me gently from my 'trance'. It became obvious that the wood was full of walkers - families with dogs mostly, so it might be difficult to concentrate because of the noise etc. - we'll see. It was more difficult to find the tree than expected, it's in a part of the wood that's a bit off the beaten track, at least not on the main paths, off to the northern side, not far from the fields. Sliding about in the mud, I tried to cut across the open woodland where the leaf litter kept the open ground drier and easier to walk on. We searched for 'my' Yew. Noticed foxglove rosettes at one spot, very fine looking for January (associated ideas - heart, blood, medicine, poison), eventually found the Yew, a youngish tree (Yews can live for thousands of years) about 30ft high, spreading, no sign of berries now, but with little bundles of fresh growth of leaves at the ends of some twigs, many 'burnt' (by frost?)

I knew of the visionary, toxic properties of the sap, when sitting under Yew, which provides the gateway to the otherworld but can lead to death if you stay there too long - hence Colin's help.

I approached the tree carefully with openness and humility, seeking its permission to work with it, and felt a similar response - it was mirroring my mood and cautiously responsive to my approach. I pulled the log, which was a couple of feet away, to the base of the trunk and covered the bare spot it had been standing on with dry leaves - there were ants nests and worm holes beneath which it would be unkind to expose to the elements. I sat and leaned back against the trunk. From above my head emerged many branches which gave the impression of hardness emerging from softness, as the flesh of the trunk had creased around the branches in a way that was suggestive of coition, of birth, of a wound inflicted by piercing, of male and female, of birth and death (i.e. the whole cycle of life)

I had expected to be transported into an altered state of consciousness, but felt no more than the usual tingle in my hands and on my lips (that's new!) which I normally experience in meditating / channelling. I closed my eyes and saw the red glow of a distant cavern or volcano - as I'd been looking at the green foliage, this complementary colouring of vision would be expected. No images came, but I became aware of a bird in the canopy above me, and opened my eyes, but as I'd removed my glasses I couldn't see it clearly. It fluttered about in the branches above me and called repeated 'seep' I closed my eyes again but could only think of the bird; so I put my glasses back on to see if I could identify it. Blue tit? Coal tit? Goldcrest? Wren? It was small and stayed just outside my clear range of vision, but appeared to change colour and shape as I watched it.

I became aware of a Golden Labrador rummaging through the dry leaves on the slope opposite where I was sitting, and thought I was about to be disturbed - but I'd only just got here, please go away! Then I saw Colin coming towards me. He sat on a stump just outside the range of the Yew and spoke to rouse me, but I was fully 'there', awake, alert. I hadn't been anywhere - but when Colin said he'd been gone 20 minutes I hardly believed him, he said I must have been somewhere for the time to have passed so quickly. I looked for the bird - but it had disappeared. I stood up and noticed one red Yew berry on one branch just beside my head. I took the spray and tied a hair around the twig it had come from as an offering.

On the journey home I thought about what had happened. Not what I had expected, that's for sure - no trance (or was there), no vision, no visitation from the otherworld, at least I thought not until . . . I remembered the words of two women - a customer who told me her meditation with a Yew tree had brought her spirit guide, and Caitlin Matthews who said that whatever you love loves you - SO, was the bird who came and flew around the tree guarding the circle? Was the bird who changed colour and shape my spirit guide? I have always loved birds, I ran a bird rescue centre when I was younger, I feed them in the garden - always have, there are always birds around me . . . Wild things, singing.

On the way back I picked up a snail shell, in pinkish browns, stripy, exactly the colours of the Yew bark, and I had the twig with a bundle of new growth and one berry - new life and fruition of old life - the feeling of being on the right track - at one with the world(s), in my proper place; approval from the woods and a spirit guide - the chameleonic bird; and a knowledge gained from the work I had done with the Ogham - The Wisdom of the Trees.

*Since writing this book:*

*Old Bob at Hill Farm has died*
*Lightfoot has become a meadow, sown with grass*
*The Black Barn has been converted, and is now lived in*
*The Plantation has grown, it will soon be a wood*
*I've been told that the 'sheepfold' in the Heather chapter is actually a hide for shooting,*
*but I expect the sheep still shelter there!*

# Glossary

*In these pages I have tried to define the terms used in this book in the way I have intended the reader to understand their use in the text. Some of these terms have historically attracted interpretations full of value judgments and emotionally charged propaganda; I hope you can suspend disbelief for the time it takes to absorb some of these definitions.*

**Amulet** - A charm worn, or used, to guard against outside forces, made using materials which correspond in meaning to the intention of the charm - see Correspondences, Sympathetic Magic

**Aura** (tree's) - Emanating from every living being is an area of subtle life force, like a spirit body, which can be felt or seen by anyone with heightened awareness as a change in the feel of the atmosphere, or as a coloured halo surrounding the whole person, animal, tree etc. This can be developed by training and practice

**Baal fires** - Fires lit for the festivals of Old Midsummer are called Baalfire. Baal was the Sun God from the ancient Middle East; Beal, Belinus and Apollo Beline were also Sun Gods, who may have been manifestations of the same deity which had travelled with the migration of people around the ancient world. Great fires were lit to celebrate many of the festivals of the Celtic year, including Beltane (1st May, meaning in the Irish language "Bel's fire"), the beginning of summer, and around the solstice when summer is at its height. Using the principal of sympathetic magic, fires were lit to encourage the Sun to shine for the ripening of the summer's crops.

**Bird Ogham** - The Ogham system evolved incorporating codes of trees, hand gestures, colours, birds etc. each list corresponding to the different letters and numbers. For birds see correspondences listed in each chapter.

**Centering** - The practice of 'tuning in' to the spiritual plane. - see Heather, Chapter 18

**Clouty Tree** - A tree, often Hawthorn, to which may be tied a Votive Offering, usually a strip of cloth, or "clout", in the hope of a cure from disease or the answer to a request.

**Correspondences** - Lists of objects, properties, mythological characters etc. which are grouped together for their corresponding meanings and interpretations.

**Cycle of Life** - The eternal progression of birth, life, death and regeneration of all beings in the physical dimension.

**Diuretic** - Stimulates urine flow.

**Druid** - Priest of the Old Religion of the Celtic people. Druids were educated over extended periods to be proficient in language and poetry, esoteric knowledge, politics and the law. They were law givers and very influential as advisors to Kings.

**Eight Festivals** - In modern Paganism, the Celtic year is divided into eight seasons focusing on the great Sabbats. Each of these was celebrated in ancient times although there is little if any evidence that they were part of a single unified system. Each festival was celebrated for a season of from one, three or twelve days to as much as a month.

*Imbolc*, 1st/2nd February, celebrating the birth of lambs, ewe's milk, and dedicated to the Celtic Goddess Brigid.

*Spring Equinox*, 21st March, the Germanic Goddess Eostra's festival, at the point of balance between light and dark in spring, when day and night are of equal length. Celebrated with eggs and leaping Hares.

*Beltane*, 1st May, Mayday, the coming of summer, the Green Man's feast. The return of fertility to the land.

*Summer Solstice*, 21st June, the longest day, the triumph of the Sun and the beginning of his decline.

*Lammas*, 1st August, the celebration of the harvest of grain.

*Autumn Equinox*, 21st September, the harvest of fruit and the bounty of the earth.

*Samhain*, 31st October/1st November, Halloween, the harvest of meat, when the animals which were not to be kept through the winter were slaughtered.

*Winter Solstice*, 21st December, the shortest day and the rebirth of the sun.

**Elements** - Air (East), Fire (South), Water (West), Earth (North) and Spirit.

**Fairies** - Not the pretty pink flying Barbie dolls of children's books, but the nature spirits which live all around us. They may be associated with or guardians of a place (sometimes called a Wight), or a particular tree or plant (Dryad), or resident of a home as a household spirit. They are not at our command, but an offering may be made with a request for their help, and some people develop communication and a kind of relationship with them over time. Not to be taken for granted, they have a keen sense of humour and some can be spiteful if provoked, a bit like us, but different.

**Feare folk** - see Fairies

**Infusion, tissane** - Just like making tea, but with herbs, using flowers or leaves 1 teaspoon dried or 2 teaspoons fresh herb in a cup, pour boiling water over and allow to stand for 5-10 minutes. Add honey to sweeten if required.

**Largesse** - This was once both the practice and the result of demanding money or food and drink with menaces, but now means generous benefaction. Can mean anything between or a combination of these two!

**Light half / dark half of the year** - During the summer months the daytime is longer than the night time, during the winter months the night time is longer than the daytime. At the Spring and Autumn Equinoxes the length of day and night are exactly equal. The light and dark halves of the year may mean from Equinox to Equinox, or sometimes these are said to change at Mayday and Halloween.

**Liminal Space** - The magical space between two states, neither one thing nor the other, but the point of stillness between. The Celts believed that in all such places were the gateways to the Other world and were therefore sacred, e.g. thresholds, between inside and outside; shorelines, between sea and land; dawn and dusk, between night and day, etc.

**Lunar month** - The time it takes for the moon to make one full circuit of the earth, approximately 28 days.

**Magic** - Forget conjuring tricks, this is real. Magic is the manipulation of events in the physical realm by the force of one's will. In practical terms, it is the focusing and directing of spiritual power by means of intention or altering the state of mind to achieve the desired change. Doctors call it the "Placebo Effect"; Christians would call it the answer to a prayer.

**Mundane world** - The physical realm, as opposed to the spiritual

**Ogham stick** - A stick cut from a living tree (having first asked the tree's permission) and inscribed with the Ogham symbol of that particular tree. Ogham sticks may be used to communicate with the spirit of the tree for divination or shamanic purposes.

**Old Religion** - The term used to describe the pre-Christian belief systems of the British Isles which have survived in the forms of superstitions, folklore and legends to the present day. Paganism

**Old Ways** - The practices of the Old Religion. Medicinal herbalism, weather lore, household craft, magic etc

**Other world** - The parallel dimension of spirit which can be accessed through practices such as meditation, shamanic journeying etc

**Paganism** - Modern paganism is a group of nature-based religions, celebrating the passage of the seasons as the "Wheel of the Year", and venerating the Divine in all things.

**Pentagram** - A five pointed star, often within a circle, consisting of a single line which begins and ends in the same place, an eternal figure linking the Elements within the circle of unity. A symbol of some modern Pagan religions. See Elements.

**Quabbalah** - The Jewish tree of life. A diagrammatic representation of the universe as layers of existence emanating from the Divine A system of concealed mystery, it is said that the knowledge of creation is to be found by meditating upon the Quabbalah or Kabbalah.

**Shamanic journey** - A journey undertaken within the spirit plane by means of altered states of consciousness, when one's own spirit roams the Other world, often with the help of a spirit guide.

**Spirit realm / plane** - see Other world

**Superstition** - Literally; super = over, statis = stands; beliefs that have been "left over" from a previous time, things that are believed or done, but no-one knows why. Often there was once a perfectly logical reason, but as times change, the understanding fades until the meaning has completely degraded.

**Sympathetic Magic** - The belief that a desired outcome may be brought about by imitation, e.g. easing childbirth by unlocking and opening the doors, windows and cupboards in the expectant mother's vicinity; or by affecting a related object, e.g. wart charming - by rubbing a piece of bacon fat on the wart, then burying it as the moon begins to wane, the "evil" is transferred to the fat, which rots more quickly due to the diminishing of the moon, when the fat has rotted away, the wart is cured! It may be that the actions actually bring about the change of mind set necessary to achieve real transformation, a recognized psychological effect used by GPs every day! Also see Magic.

**Tincture** - Dissolving the active ingredients of herbs in alcohol gives a stronger product than does an infusion, and may be stored for up to two years. To make a tincture, fill a sterile glass jar with 4oz dried or 6oz fresh chopped herb, and pour over 1pint vodka (35% - 40% alcohol). Shake well for 2mins. Store in a cool, dark place for 14 days, shaking every day. Strain the tincture through muslin into a sterile dark glass jar, label and store in a cool, dark place. The standard dose is 1 teaspoon tincture in 5 teaspoons water 2-3 times a day.

**Tissane** - see Infusion.

**Votive Offering** - An offering, made in the hope of receiving an answer to a request, perhaps an object precious to the supplicant, or a representation of the request itself. Pilgrims to a holy well in search of a cure would throw in a coin or dip a strip of cloth into the water and rub it on the affected part, then tie it to an overhanging tree, partly to maintain the mystical link between the well and the supplicant, but as the "clout" rotted away, the disease was believed to be healed. Some "Clouty trees" were also the recipients of dolls' limbs, or other images of the part of the body for which a cure was sought. See also Sympathetic Magic.

**Web of Wyrd** - The Celts believed that all things in both the physical and spiritual realms are interconnected by a huge web, which allows the adept to "read" or affect distantly, enabling clairvoyance and magic.

**Wise Woman / Cunning Man** - A country healer or herbalist, midwife and layer out of the dead. Sometimes thought to possess magical powers, which people sought for spells to improve their lot, e.g. love potions. Wise and cunning people were not above taking advantage of the gullible and desperate!

**Witch** - Sometimes a fantasy character in an old story; sometimes a Wise Woman, as often the "craft of the wise" was misunderstood and demonized by the Church; when the Witch Finders were about in C17 (Matthew Hopkins et al) it could be anyone who was denounced by their neighbours for political reasons, as, if the trial was successful, the witch finder and the accuser both benefited from the division of the "witches" property!

**World Axis** - The imaginary pillar or tree around which all of reality hangs, connecting the underworld, the physical world we live in and the heavens.

**Yggdrasil** - The Norse Cosmic Tree, or World Axis which is the foundation of all reality. It supports the worlds of Men, Giants, light and dark Elves, the underworld, and the realm of the Gods. Usually refered to as an Ash tree, but some now think that the Germanic name for a Yew, meaning "Needle-Ash", suggests that it may have actually been a Yew tree.

**Yule** - The pre-Christian festival of midwinter. The birthday of the Sun, when the days begin to lengthen and the sun's power starts to return. Incidentally, the early Celtic Christian monks venerated the sun believing it to be the face of God; they had a lovely way of incorporating the old pagan beliefs into the new religion and could see no contradiction between the two.

# Botanical Glossary

**Alder carr** - A group of Alder trees, usually standing together on a river bank. Alder seeds fall into the water and travel downstream, where they lodge in mud on the bank and grow.

**Bud, axil** - A bud growing in the fork between a branch and a leaf stalk.

**Bud, terminal** - A bud at the growing tip of a branch.

**Catkins** - drooping tassels of flowers.

**Coppice, Coppiced** - A tree cut down to just above ground level every 3 to 5 years or so. New growth emerges from the resulting "stool" as long rods. Used to produce the raw materials for hurdles, baskets etc. Coppicing allows a tree to regenerate for extended periods, sometimes centuries.

**Crab Apple** - The native tree from which cultivated apple trees were derived.

**Deciduous** - Trees which shed their leaves each year.

**Leaf, paired** - Leaves or leaflets that emerge opposite one another on the stem.

**Leaf, serrated** - Leaf with a saw-toothed margin.

**Node** - growth site, bearing a bud or a scar.

**Ovule** - (flower part) Unfertilized, potential seed.

**Pollard, Pollarded** - A tree cut at a height of about 6-12 feet above the ground to produce new growth all at the same level, for successive crops of wood.

**Pollen** - Male reproductive cell, fertilizes female ovule.

**Pussywillows** - Whitish fluffy buds commonly seen on Willow trees, and others, during spring.

**Stamen** - (flower part) Male fertilizing organ, bearing pollen

**Stigma** - (flower part) Receptacle of the female reproductive organ.

# Notes

# Index

# Index of Deities & Mythology

*From ancient times all civilizations mentioned in this book have believed in some form of deity or deities. Many ancient peoples venerated a Great Mother Goddess. Some adopted a pantheon of Gods and Goddesses, who may at times have interbred with mortal humans, producing offspring with superhuman characteristics, and thought to be semi divine. Mythologies have evolved which may be encoded history and which tell of the deeds of Gods and Heroes, both mortal and divine. As monotheism developed, the idea of the Father God emerged, eventually evolving into the Christian Trinity. In this book I have used the word "deity" to mean all of these concepts, where a personality is venerated by a group of people, and held to be divine or semi divine, usually for their particular attributes and associations.*

# Notes

# Notes

# Notes

# Notes

also by Karen Cater:

# spirit of the hare
## in folklore, mythology & the artist's landscape

Folklore, Mythology, Customs, Songs, Stories,
Art, Mysticism, Superstitions.
Diary pages describing Karen's encounters with hares.
Full colour illustrations throughout -
watercolours, linocuts, drawings & photographs.

available from www.hedinghamfair.co.uk
**ISBN 978-0-9556475-3-6**
**www.hedinghamfair.co.uk**

For a long time Karen Cater has been intrigued by the mystical Hare, springing up in visual images seemingly for centuries. From boxing hares by the light of the moon to the mysterious Triple Hare, the so called 'Tinners Rabbits'. Everywhere there were Hares. She was determined to discover why hares have held such fascination for creative people and set out to explore their significance. Gradually she uncovered a rich seem of mythology drawn from all over the world, from the earliest

creation myths at the very dawn of time.

The Hare is the bringer of light and particularly in European traditions also symbolises fertility. After the Witch hysteria of the 17th century had died down the Hare became associated with bad luck, but its attraction has persisted in latter-day folklore and beyond into modern psychology. Legends came with stories, songs and images that spoke to the deepest parts of Karen's consciousness. Where would they lead her? Her magical voyage of discovery unfolds through the pages of this beautifully illustrated journal.

Visit the Hares that live in the fields around Karen's home. Experience the seasons of their life and the changing fortunes and fashions that hares everywhere have endured over the centuries, but above all, discover the message that the hare has for us in the modern world; a message of hope and a promise of peace.

All the illustrations in this book are by Karen Cater
Many of them are available as greetings cards, mounted prints,
or as T-shirt designs from

edingham
Fair

for a free illustrated catalogue:
www.hedinghamfair.co.uk
01787 462731